Eva Schilke

WHEN
THE
KINGDOM
COMES

D1622208

Steve Gray, with a B.M.E. from Central Missouri State University, is founder and senior pastor of Smithton (Missouri) Community Church. An ordained minister, gifted speaker and musician, Steve has pastored the church since May 1984. God came like lightning into the Sunday evening service on March 24, 1996, and transformed the church. Currently it holds five services a week.

In 1999 Hosanna/Integrity Music recorded a worship CD of original Smithton songs, and Steve recorded a solo CD.

Steve and his wife, Kathy, have one grown daughter and live in Smithton, a town of fewer than 600 people.

To contact Pastor Steve Gray for speaking engagements or to order the many teaching tapes available, you may write or call:

Pastor Steve Gray
P.O. Box 430
Smithton, MO 65350
(660) 343-5437
(877) 804-LIFE

WHEN THE KINGDOM COMES

Lessons from the Smithton Outpouring

Steve Gray

Foreword by Stephen Hill

Chosen Books

A Division of Baker Book House Co
Grand Rapids, Michigan 49516

© 1999 by Steve Gray

Published by Chosen Books
a division of Baker Book House Company
P.O. Box 6287, Grand Rapids, MI 49516-6287

Second printing, November 1999

Printed in the United States of America

All rights reserved. No part of this publication may be reproduced, stored in a retrieval system, or transmitted in any form or by any means—for example, electronic, photocopy, recording—without the prior written permission of the publisher. The only exception is brief quotations in printed reviews.

Library of Congress Cataloging-in-Publication Data

Gray, Steve, 1952–
    When the kingdom comes: lessons from the Smithton
outpouring / Steve Gray.
       p.   cm.
    ISBN 0-8007-9271-8 (pbk.)
    1. Revivals. I. Title.
    BV3790.G75   1999
    269—dc21   99-17004

Unless otherwise noted, Scripture quotations are taken from the HOLY BIBLE, NEW INTERNATIONAL VERSION®. NIV®. Copyright © 1973, 1978, 1984 by International Bible Society. Used by permission of Zondervan Publishing House. All rights reserved.

Scripture quotations marked KJV are from the King James Version of the Bible.

For current information about all releases from Baker Book House, visit our web site:
                         http://www.bakerbooks.com

Contents

To my dear wife, Kathy, who taught me to be singleminded for Jesus in a doubleminded world.

To my daughter, Bobbie, who taught me unconditional love.

To my wonderful father- and mother-in-law, Bob and Jeanne Moffatt, because you prayed and believed.

Foreword

STEVE and Kathy Gray, well known for their role as the pastors of Smithton Community Church in Smithton, Missouri, have experienced a genuine touch from God, and stand as testimonies to what the Lord will do for sincere, hungry believers.

While reading this book, I found a six-word statement that serves as a foundation for what is taking place in their church. Pastor Steve makes it plain when he writes, "We wanted God no matter what." This one sentence is a strong declaration of spiritual hunger. It is the cry of a people who have abandoned themselves to God.

Revival, you see, will never be found on the bargain table. There are no discounts. It is expensive; it will cost you everything. Also, true revival comes from above and is not affected by human scrutiny and cross-examination. It comes to those who are truly hungry for a touch from God. Over the years I have met many who claim to be hungry for God, but their hunger seems always to be coupled with conditions. They want God, but on their terms. They want Jesus Christ to be the Lord of their lives, but only to the extent that they do not have to relinquish personal control. They want the Holy Spirit to come in power, but they do not want their secure social standing to be jeopardized. Friend, that is not hunger!

The Bible states clearly in Matthew 5:6, "Blessed are they which do hunger and thirst after righteousness: for they shall be filled" (KJV). This hunger has to do with an all-consuming craving for God. A man's desperation for the presence of God should melt all preoccupation with self, fame, public image and social status. His hunger and thirst, if genuine, will drive him to eat and drink regardless of the opinions of others. He will be willing to be a fool in the sight of his peers in order to be embraced in the arms of the Lord. This is the attitude of the pastors and members of Smithton Community Church. They wanted God no matter what!

I have had the distinct privilege of ministering with Steve and Kathy. Their relationship with Jesus is real, their worship is fresh and their zeal for God is contagious. Reader, you will find these same elements throughout *When the Kingdom Comes*. Be prepared for a down-to-earth, easy-to-understand, up-front, in-your-face adventure. Pastor Steve will show you where revival comes from, what it will do for your church and part of the price you will pay. This is not a how-to book; rather, it contains a real story, with real people, in a real church, nestled in a real community. It is the story of how a real and loving God touched their lives and how they will never be the same.

Pastor Steve Gray will take you on a ride past stale, dry religion into a heaven-sent outpouring of God's Spirit. You will examine the foundation of revival and gain a solid understanding of why God chose to pour out His Spirit.

Welcome to Smithton, Missouri—a place perhaps insignificant in man's eyes, but holy ground in the eyes of God. Welcome to the Smithton Outpouring!

Stephen L. Hill, evangelist
Brownsville Revival
Pensacola, Florida

Acknowledgments

I would like to thank Joel Kilpatrick for his help in writing this book and his excellent guidance in the craft of writing until I could finally form a sentence on my own. Joel shared his gift of writing with unselfish zeal, and because of his talent and encouragement, the message of the Smithton Outpouring can now be shared with the world.

I also would like to thank Jane Campbell for her wisdom as an editor. Her excitement kept me inspired and helped me believe that the lessons of this book were needed in the Body of Christ.

Part 1

The Kingdom of God Is at Hand

The Inbreaking Kingdom

THE road home looked painfully familiar as I drove up Highway 65 in the pouring rain. As I headed back to Smithton Community Church in March 1996 for the Sunday evening service, I knew I was at a threshold in my life. Either something would change and God would somehow break through, or else I would leave the ministry and try to put the pieces back together some other way.

I was at the lowest point of my life. After pastoring for twelve years in a small, country church in rural Missouri, I had reached the breaking point and no longer wanted to be a pastor. Bruised and cut by many seasons of intentional hurt, gossip and mistrust, I had watched as my passion for ministry had been suffocated. My faith in people was nearly destroyed, my faith in myself utterly gone. I felt crushed and unusable, worthless and wounded beyond repair. I had tried my best but believed God was finished with me.

At the recommendation of my wife, Kathy, I had taken a two-week break from ministry to see if I could somehow find and meet with the living God. It was hard to know where to go—and worse yet, what if nothing happened?

I had heard of a revival happening down in Florida. I did not really expect much, but it was at least a place to land for a few days.

The hours driving were lonely and dismal. I felt as though all the hope and life had drained out of me. I kept thinking what a miserable failure I had become—at least on the inside, where it really counted.

After checking into a motel, I sat in the empty room and stared at the walls. I had never felt such aloneness. I tried to pray but it felt as though a bunch of empty words were falling to the floor.

When the time came, I found my way to the Brownsville Assembly of God church and wandered in. There were few seats left, and I sat accidentally in a reserved section (for the handicapped, I think). *Great,* I thought. *At any moment someone will come and ask me to leave.* Then I noticed a seat over against the wall and moved quickly to it. There I sat as the service started, listening to happy, excited people give testimonies describing what had happened to them and how their church had changed.

I don't remember what the sermon was about that night, but at the end of the service I responded to the altar call and went to a corner of the stage steps to pray. A man nearby was dressed in a nice, three-piece suit, kneeling and crying as hard as I have ever heard any man. At first I thought he must have committed some really big sin. But as I watched him, I realized he had what I needed. This man was completely broken. I wanted this more than anything else. I joined him and cried, too, as I listened to him pour out his heart before God.

I spent the next few days trying to get a breakthrough from heaven, and I spent the next few nights at church. Nothing changed. Then one afternoon I played a cassette tape and heard a song I had never heard before. The words were like a wrenching from my heart—"Everything is in your hands, O God"—and something finally broke. For the first time, hope came in. I called Kathy and told her, "I feel like I just got saved."

I went to the service that night, realizing I had not spoken face to face with anyone for days. Suddenly, while sitting in the balcony, I heard what I thought might be the Lord speaking to me: *I want you to have a revival.* It was the most ridiculous thing a man in my condition could have heard! Watching as others flooded the altar, crying out for revival in their churches, I did not even know if I belonged in the ministry anymore.

I put what I might have heard from God out of my mind.

I spent the entire next day in prayer. That night I heard the same thing: *I want you to have a revival.* It made no sense at all. How could I have a revival? I was broken and in pieces and had nothing to preach to anyone. Again I tried to forget about it.

During the next service, it happened a third time: *I want you to have a revival.* It could not have felt more odd—looking at the move of God happening in front of me and feeling so far from where those people were. How could I bring a revival to anyone?

But this time the voice came with a correction. *I didn't say you had to be a revival. I said I want you to have a revival.*

This made sense to me. As long as I did not have to be the revival, all I had to do was show up and see what God would do.

Two weeks after arriving in Florida, I took my time driving the back roads to Smithton, thinking of little else. What if nothing changed? What if I had made all this up?

How many others had prayed specifically for revival, while I had never even asked?

I drove into Smithton with mixed feelings. It is a village so small it does not appear on many maps. There are no traffic lights, no restaurants, no gas stations—not even a soda machine. To spend any money, you have to drive to Sedalia ten miles away. Kathy and I had been called there by the Lord to resurrect a church, and through the years we had built a good core of 150 people who were faithful with their attendance and their tithes. They had trusted me as their leader, had listened to me preach, had given us their friendship. They were the ones I felt I would betray if I gave it all up.

I arrived at church and pulled the car into the same parking space I had used for twelve years. With some hesitation I opened the outer door of the white-paneled country church building we occupied—so classic in appearance that it could have leaped off a Currier & Ives print. The oldest church building in the county, it was still held together with wooden pegs.

I could hear the sounds of worship coming through the antique walls. I pushed open the sanctuary door behind the platform. There was Kathy in the front row. The people were singing and clapping. The familiar atmosphere enfolded me like a warm blanket. Kathy grinned, and I decided to walk over and give her a hug as my first act as returning pastor. She had just looked at her watch, apparently wondering when I was going to arrive. It was 6:12 P.M.

I took about eight steps toward her. Then, with astounding suddenness and great intensity, a bolt of spiritual power hit me. I felt as though I had been struck by lightning. My arms shot up into the air, the emotional weights flew off my shoulders and I began to jump up and down and twirl as I had never done in my life. I felt indescribable joy and hope and a lightness about life that had never been so strong, even when I was baptized in the Holy Spirit twenty years before.

It did not hit only me. The bolt of heaven-sent electricity seemed to shoot off in individual tributaries and strike everyone in the church all at the same time. People began to leap. Many rushed forward. We all were jumping up and down, dancing and laughing, having the best time we had ever had together, and we had no idea what had caused it—other than the Lord—or why it was happening.

A little while later I tried to share a message with the congregation. But although I was thinking with amazing clarity, my mouth would not work. Words would not come out right. So rather than stammer and stutter, I decided to be pastoral and simply pray for people. I did not lay hands on a single person. But when I lifted up my hands to approach them, they started collapsing and crying. Their repentance and brokenness were evident. I had done nothing extraordinary, and was puzzled and full of awe.

What is God doing? I wondered. *What does this mean?*

We did not know what to call it, what it was or why it had come. I had not been looking for revival; I had been looking for survival! I had only wanted to get through each day without my heart collapsing. But at the end of the service in March 1996, I announced that I was coming back the next night to pray and seek God, and anyone who wanted to join me was welcome.

The entire congregation showed up. As we worshiped and prayed, the same awesome presence of God came in on us. At the end of the gathering I invited everyone back again.

As often as we came, the same Presence was there. By the third week outsiders began to come and word began to spread. Revival had come to Smithton. Soon we began to realize this was the moment we had been born for. This was why we were created.

Since then my life has never been the same. Even though I had been filled with God's Spirit for more than twenty years, I discovered an experience of God's power extending beyond anything I have ever known. The Kingdom of God broke in on our church forcefully—not just once but over and over. What did it change? Absolutely everything.

Listen for the Window

We are living in a day of the inbreaking Kingdom. The Kingdom of God is breaking forcefully into people's lives and churches just as it did when Jesus walked the earth. It may have broken into your life or the life of someone you know. It may have broken into your church, your Bible study, your denomination. Or perhaps you are hearing these rumors of glory for the first time, but in your heart you have a yearning for God such as you have never known. The fact is, the Kingdom is breaking through to people around the world. Whether they call it revival or renewal, reformation or revolution, outpouring or the first rumblings of spiritual awakening, it is changing the entire picture of what it means to be a follower of Christ.

When I was a boy my mother would open an upstairs window and call for my brother and me to come inside. The sound of the window was as familiar as the sound of our mother's voice. The screech as it opened was message enough; the voice that followed was hardly needed.

My brother and I could have ignored our mother's summons. We could have argued with her, especially if she had interrupted our game. We could even have run away and played in someone else's yard. But when we obeyed and went inside, we always found that Mom's plan was better than ours. Maybe she had dinner ready, or maybe it was getting cold outside, or maybe we had to do our homework. We learned to respect her timing and to obey. That experience symbolizes to me how God's people can respond when He opens the window to call for us. Will we pretend we did not hear? Will we turn defiantly the other way? Will we stand and argue? Or will we trust His providence and watch His magnificent plan unfold? Interestingly the Bible shows us a common response from God's people when He calls. In this pattern some leaders of existing religious systems get extremely uncomfortable because they do not want to respond or obey. Why does this happen? I do not know, but it is clear that it does. Many of the Pharisees were incensed over Jesus' ministry—not because He was setting people free, healing their bodies and leading them to the Father, but because He claimed that the Kingdom was breaking in and that, in their blindness, the Pharisees could not see it. Their religion bound them. They were trapped into defending what they knew because they feared what they did not recognize. They were servants not of the Kingdom but of a religious system. They did not recognize the lifting of the window.

When God breaks in we realize that everything we considered religious was not necessarily God. When the Kingdom breaks through, many outcasts and nobodies are raised up to lead. We may be shocked by the people who are called, but God has a habit of making nobodies somebodies. Think of the stories in the Bible that demonstrate this—stories about Abraham, David, Jeremiah, Nehemiah. When His Kingdom breaks in, God picks up the pieces, the leftovers and the left-outs and makes them powerful in His service.

Jesus demonstrated this further by going to the blind and the lame and the lepers. We marvel that He healed them, but we often miss the more substantial point. Those people were not just blind and lame and full of leprosy; they were outcasts of Israel, not allowed to exercise full membership as covenant believers (as it were) in the Kingdom of God. When Jesus, the embodiment of the inbreaking Kingdom, began touching them, He was not just healing the unclean, blemished people of God; He was restoring their membership and participation in God's family.

We live in a day when God is once more opening the window of heaven and calling out to His children to receive full membership in the Kingdom. This is one of the most amazing and critical times in all history—a time when the power of God is being restored to the Church, when outcasts are being raised up to lead, when glitz and glamour are being purged, when families are coming back together under the headship of Christ. What makes it even more staggering is the fact that this is the first time in two thousand years that worldwide revival has broken out while Israel is a nation. The last time Israel had an opportunity as a nation to embrace the inbreaking Kingdom was when Jesus walked the earth and shortly thereafter. That opportunity ended in A.D. 70 when Rome destroyed Jerusalem and scattered the Jewish people.

This, then, is our opportunity. The Kingdom of God has arrived. We must abandon everything to pursue it, treating it like the lost coin, the treasure in the field, the pearl of great price. We have the occasion to achieve right now more than a person could normally accomplish with a thousand lives to live! We can be part of the eternal Kingdom of God as it breaks into our dimension of time and space.

What Is the Kingdom of God?

How can we understand the Kingdom of God? In Mark 4:11 Jesus said that "the secret [or mystery] of the kingdom of God" had been given to those listening. To understand what Jesus meant, we have to understand the Jewish minds of His audience.

For centuries the Jews had expected the Kingdom to come to them. Their expectation rested on a King David type of king and an Elijah type of messiah who would defeat all Israel's oppressors and, through the Jews, rule the earth.

Although Jesus claimed that the Kingdom had arrived, it did not come in the way Israel expected. Instead it came as a mustard seed, its arrival barely noticed by the rest of the world. Yet it did arrive and would grow, until its final burst of power at the judging of the nations.

How easy it is to miss a tiny seed or a little leaven that will eventually permeate the entire loaf! Consequently the religious folks of Jesus' day were no more aware of the presence of God's Kingdom than most of the modern Church is today. It comes as a secret and ends in judgment of the nations.

As the Kingdom arrived, it brought with it signs of God's rule and God's favor. The powers of darkness were signaled from heaven that, for them, the beginning of the end had come. The full Kingdom of the future had broken into the present. It came with visible signs of healing, power and deliverance that anyone could see. The greatest effect of this now-planted seed Kingdom was the invisible presence that opens spiritual eyes and hearts and minds.

In the end God's Kingdom will come in fullness, and the King, Jesus Christ, will reign with a rod of iron. But for now the Kingdom rules through volunteers. It calls those volunteers to orient their entire lives around it and to seek it as first priority.

The Pharisees missed the Kingdom because it did not come or look the way they expected. Nevertheless it was within their reach.

Many people over the years have gotten off-track in their understanding of the Kingdom because Jesus told the Pharisees in Luke 17:21 that "the kingdom of God is within you." It makes no sense—so believe these people—to say such a thing to the same group to whom Jesus also said, "You belong to your father, the devil" (John 8:44).

But to make a doctrine from one Scripture is foolish when the Bible is so full of Kingdom statements. Obviously the Kingdom does not reside in just anyone, nor is that what Jesus wanted His hearers to know. Rather He wanted them to understand that although the Kingdom may not come in the way you or I expect, it is here just the same—and it is within your reach!

We live in a day when the Kingdom of God, which long seemed distant and far away, has once again broken into the lives of God's people. The Kingdom is within the reach of any church or any person who will give himself to it.

God's rule and reign and work have again become active. It takes faith to cooperate, because His is an invisible Kingdom with an invisible King. Those of faith who will receive the Kingdom and give absolute loyalty to the King will be rewarded. Those who reject it or are too preoccupied with the kingdom of this world will suffer the consequences when God's Kingdom comes in all its fullness.

As long as the Kingdom lay in the distance, we could coast along down the middle of the road. But now, as we approach the end of the last days, God has started in again with signs and wonders and healings and deliverance. The distant and sometimes seemingly dormant Kingdom has again become active, so that all people everywhere can respond with sincere hearts and usher in the glory of God and the final return of the Son of Man.

Kingdom People

During these days when thousands of Kingdom people are being gathered all over the world, it seems to me that Jesus is saying once again, "Come to me, all you who are weary and burdened, and I will give you rest" (Matthew 11:28).

This may not seem like the message we would expect to hear since, traditionally, it is used as an evangelistic invitation to unbelievers. It is often presented to those uninterested in serving God but who are weary from serving themselves and the world.

Although those individuals need to hear the message, I do not believe they are the ones Jesus was addressing. I believe it was a call to the Jews who had been trying to serve God and who had worn themselves out in their own strength. It was not a call to "yokeless" people but to those weary from carrying the yoke of trying to find the living God; to those weary of religion without the power or presence of God. They needed rest for their souls because, as hard as they tried, they could not find Him by themselves.

Jesus calls such weary followers to Himself to get rid of the yoke of the current national religion and take His yoke upon them. He offers Himself to them along with His way of living and serving. With our own yoke, we try to get to God, but with His yoke, God comes to us.

It reminds me of David in the cave at Adullam. While there he was joined by those who were in distress or in debt or in discontent. Why had they left the comforts of home to live in a cave, and why were they in such distress and discontent? They had left to escape the corrupt reign of King Saul. It was not that Saul was never meant to be king, but he became corrupt and disobedient and murderous. They were not only distressed by the system and indebted to it, but they were discontented with a kingdom that no longer enjoyed God's blessing.

They did not just walk out on their past; they joined themselves to the new future. They wanted to be part of the next move of God and to join themselves to the future king. Eventually they would become David's mighty men and be blessed of the Lord again.

God is gathering up Kingdom people once more. These are the people distressed with dead religion that has lost the presence of God. They are worn out by indebtedness to sins that they were promised would no longer have power over them. They are discontented by churches with little real interest in the living God and that are filled with division, carnality and the works of the flesh. They are worn out with self-help and self-improvement preaching while the spiritual condition of the Church declines.

They have listened and tried and now they are exhausted and want out of a corrupt system that mirrors the days of King Saul and the religious Pharisees of Jesus' day. These people want to see the return of the glory of God and walk with the living God. They do not want to be told that everything is all right when sin is crouching at our doors, and oppression, depression, suicide, drugs, division, greed, pride and the entire system of the world sits in our pews and stands in our pulpits.

You bet we are worn out and discontented and in distress! We feel the call to a glorious, radiant church full of people who really love each other and want nothing more from this life than to spend it with Jesus.

To them, to you, to us, the Kingdom is coming and breaking into our lives with great force and power. Just as David's men left the comforts of home, so our lives are being rearranged and our religion transformed, because Jesus is bringing the Kingdom near to ordinary people again. We will never possess the Kingdom fully in this life.

But it is nearer now than before, and the same signs and wonders and presence of God are coming again, much in the same way as in Israel two thousand years ago.

We find three helpful and important glimpses at the approach of revival in the book of 2 Kings. The first picture comes from 2 Kings 2:19–22. In this story we are told that the city has a spring of water but that the water has gone bad. Elisha comes to them and throws salt into the spring. Immediately the water is healed.

This is how it will be for many today. Someone who walks in the power of revival will come to you and your church and "salt" the bad water until it is healed. This is the more traditional way for us to receive.

The second glimpse of revival is found in 2 Kings 3:17, where God miraculously fills the valley with water and everyone comes to drink. No one really does anything; the Word of God is spoken and the hand of the Lord does the work. It is not "normal." There was neither wind nor rain, but suddenly the dry valley is flowing with living water. This is the way most of us would like revival to come.

The last way is sometimes the hardest. In 2 Kings 5:1–14 Naaman, a valiant soldier, has leprosy. What will bring his healing? He must go to someone else's river and dip himself seven times. Naaman does not like the idea at all. He gets angry, like many today, and wants to know why he cannot just dip himself in his own river. After all, his rivers are better, anyway!

I have seen many others make the same mistake as Naaman. "Why do I have to go someplace else to find revival? Our church is better, anyway! Why can't God just do it in our church?" I don't always have the answer to those questions, but for some, obedience is what God is looking for.

The logic brought forth in the story of the Syrian commander is remarkable and reveals our human nature. The servants tell Naaman, "If you were told to do something hard, you would do it." We sometimes stumble at the easy things: "Just go and be washed and be cleansed." Finally the soldier goes and dips himself seven times, and is restored.

Maybe God will send someone. Maybe God will do it all by Himself. Maybe you need to go to another river to be restored. Whichever way God decides, it is clear that He is sweetening the waters, filling our valleys and restoring our flesh.

If you are discontented with your spiritual walk and distressed by all you see around you, then read on. When the Kingdom comes, the glory and presence of the Lord return to the people of God—and everything changes.

The Promised Church

One day as he was teaching the people in the temple courts and preaching the gospel, the chief priests and the teachers of the law, together with the elders, came up to him. "Tell us by what authority you are doing these things," they said. "Who gave you this authority?" He replied, "I will also ask you a question. Tell me, John's baptism—was it from heaven, or from men?" They discussed it among themselves and said, "If we say, 'From heaven,' he will ask, 'Why didn't you believe him?' But if we say, 'From men,' all the people will stone us, because they are persuaded that John was a prophet." So they answered, "We don't know where it was from." Jesus said, "Neither will I tell you by what authority I am doing these things."

Luke 20:1–8

IN this season of revival God is showing us that not everything going on in our churches, regardless of what flies on the banners above, passes the test. In an atmosphere of repentance many of us have found ungodly things within ourselves. So, too, we are beginning to find ungodly things in the institutions we have built.

As we learn from Jeremiah 51:9 (which we will look at in a minute), God's pattern is to uproot, tear down and destroy before He rebuilds. And before the Kingdom can be further built up, many manmade structures have to be torn down. God has been gracious in giving us the opportunity to clean house and reorder our lives rather than bringing the swift judgment we deserve.

In the New Testament passage quoted above, we find one of many confrontations between the Pharisees and Jesus. They asked Him, "By what authority are You doing these things?" It was not Jesus' preaching or healing or miracles alone that pushed the Pharisees to take His life, but the fact that He disrupted the established order of Temple operations, overturning the tables and driving out the money-changers. This horrified and infuriated the Pharisees, who demanded that Jesus prove His authority to challenge centuries-old traditions with such a raw and emotional display.

We often refer to this incident as the cleansing of the Temple, but that is misleading. This was no once-over with a feather duster; it was not even a spring cleaning. Jesus was giving a living, prophetic picture—violent, rowdy and entirely impolite—of what God was going to do to the Temple some forty years later through Roman conquest. At that date God would not come and cleanse the Temple; He would cause it to be destroyed. Jesus foretold this by upsetting the furniture and the financial network that had grown up around the religious rituals.

When God actually destroyed the Temple, He did not go in with paper towels and a bottle of Windex; the entire system went down.

First, Flee from Babylon!

Many of Jesus' sermons aimed to warn people of the downfall of the old, corrupt system often referred to in the Bible as Babylon. Jeremiah 51:6–9 gives an excellent picture of this downfall:

> "Flee from Babylon! Run for your lives! Do not be destroyed because of her sins. It is time for the Lord's vengeance; he will pay her what she deserves. Babylon was a gold cup in the Lord's hand; she made the whole earth drunk. The nations drank her wine; therefore they have now gone mad. Babylon will suddenly fall and be broken. Wail over her! Get balm for her pain; perhaps she can be healed. 'We would have healed Babylon, but she cannot be healed; let us leave her and each go to his own land, for her judgment reaches to the skies, it rises as high as the clouds.'"

This Old Testament Scripture forms the backdrop for Jesus' admonitions. Babylon represented a corrupt religious system and Jeremiah predicted its doom. Normally we would expect God to encourage His people to hold on or stand firm, but here we see a religious system that cannot be healed. When religion becomes so corrupt that it cannot be healed, the only appropriate action is to take flight and run for your lives. Flight from Babylon is a recurring theme in Scripture, such as in Revelation 18:4, which sounds the warning to "come out of her, my people."

The lesson Jeremiah taught in his day, and that Jesus taught in His day, is still true in ours. Corrupt and compromised religion will fall. But out of that religion, just as in Jesus' day, comes a new and fresh group loyal to God and His Kingdom.

I received an e-mail from a pastor who said he was dying spiritually in what was known as a Spirit-filled church. This man had been touched by God and desperately wanted more, but his church would not budge. "Should I leave," he asked me, "or should I stay?"

I quoted Jeremiah 51:9 and offered this advice: "Do all you can to bring a true move of God. But if nothing changes, remember you might be dealing with a religious group so overcome by Babylon that it cannot be healed. Jesus died for those people, but we don't have to, and though we should do what we can to reach them, it is not our job to die spiritually trying to reach them."

Some months passed before I heard from this pastor again. He took my advice and did all he could, until there was nothing left he felt would make a difference. He resigned, and a week later found a church crying out for revival. Spiritually this pastor came alive again.

Some of what Jesus said about the downfall of corrupt religion is so strong that we take it out of context and, in effect, obscure its meaning. In the gospel of Mark, for example, after Jesus cursed the fig tree and cleansed the Temple, He uttered that famous line quoted by many out of context:

> "If anyone says to this mountain, 'Go, throw yourself into the sea,' and does not doubt in his heart but believes that what he says will happen, it will be done for him."
>
> Mark 11:23

If you want to be charismatic about it, you pretend this refers to the mountain of your circumstances—but that is taking the passage out of context. Jesus was not referring to the mountain of circumstances. When He referred to "this mountain," I believe (based in part on Zechariah 4:6–9) that He was looking at the Temple Mount and indicating that "the mountain on which the Temple sits is going to be removed," referring to its destruction by the Romans.

This is why Jesus also said, "Have faith in God" (verse 22)—because the day was soon coming when the Jews would walk through Jerusalem and have no Temple to admire for its magnificence. Jesus was saying, "Don't get hooked on the present-day picture, because the day is coming when not one stone will stand on another, and you will not have faith in the Temple. Nor will you have faith in your synagogue or in the Pharisees. You will have faith in God alone, because the rest isn't going to be there anymore."

Much of what Jesus said was intended to clue people in to the fact that the religious system of the day would be overthrown, but we miss much of it because we Americanize it, making it say what we want it to say. We turn the parables into fables or moral stories instead of living prophecies that pertain as much to us as to the audience that first heard them.

Here is the passage from Zechariah to which I believe Jesus alluded. If I said, "'Not by might nor by power . . .'" most believers could quote the rest of it: "'But by my Spirit,' says the LORD." But we have so stripped this verse of its context that we have no idea how it was used. We know the con-*tent* but not the con-*text*. Here is how that passage goes:

> "This is the word of the LORD to Zerubbabel: 'Not by might nor by power, but by my Spirit,' says the LORD Almighty. What are you, O mighty mountain? Before Zerubbabel you will become level ground. Then he will bring out the capstone to shouts of 'God bless it! God bless it!'" Then the word of the LORD came to me: "The hands of Zerubbabel have laid the foundation of this temple; his hands will also complete it. Then you will know that the LORD Almighty has sent me to you."
>
> Zechariah 4:6–9

If you do not know what the full passage says, you will not see that in Luke 20, when Jesus talked about a mountain being cast into the sea, He was referring to this passage in Zechariah. And when the mountain is leveled, there is to be a new capstone and a new building in its place. At the appearance of the capstone, the people shout, "God bless it!" or "Grace to you!" This whole passage is Temple talk and foreshadows the Messiah. Something will be destroyed, and it is not by might, not by power, but by God's Spirit.

Thus, in Luke 20 Jesus has just thrown a couple of Scriptures at us in context. The mighty mountain will become level ground.

But why did that mountain have to be leveled or removed? Why did those tables have to be overturned? Because the present Temple religion was an obstacle blocking the way of the new Temple. Of all the institutions that might have represented an obstacle to the Kingdom, God did not pinpoint paganism or Rome or an army. If Rome had been an obstacle, Rome would have been removed, but Rome was not removed. If the obstacle had been some military force, God would have dealt with it. But that was not the problem. The hindrance that needed to be removed was the religious system.

What Is Stopping the Inbreaking Kingdom Today?

Today the main obstacle opposing the Kingdom of God is not the government or immorality or demons or the media or crack houses, although these are major social problems. Nor is the Kingdom being hindered by God's reluctance or by bad timing on the part of the Holy Spirit. The Kingdom is being held back primarily by the present religious system that does not want it to break in and disturb things.

Everybody who has been touched by revival already knows this. People who have not said yes to revival are trying to blend the old and new. They see a few problems in the Church, so they set out to have a summit, a meeting, a congress, a committee. The old mindset wants to get together and clean the thing up, or perhaps have an all-church workday. That is why Christians like the "cleansing of the Temple" idea rather than what Jesus really did. They want to Windex the problems they see, misunderstanding the problems and underestimating the necessary response.

In every city I visit, every place I preach, every place we pray for a move of the Holy Spirit, I feel the opposition. Sure, there are principalities and powers in the spiritual realm that fight revival. They whisper lies and try to crack the foundation. But that is not primarily what stops a move of God. No, it is the people who claim to know God. They put up the stop sign and think revival is going too far.

In one city where I was preaching, the night services had been particularly powerful. Many pastors present were experiencing major life changes. The last night, however, seemed stiff. Something was not right. I was getting to the end of my sermon, and Kathy told me later she was wondering how I was going to give an altar call, because it was not going that well.

Two minutes before the end, as I took a breath, a woman at the back of the assembly of nine hundred people began to yell at me at the top of her lungs.

"You're talking to us as though we don't want the presence of God," she shouted, "as though we don't have it! You're acting as if we don't care!"

As she continued, tension hit the entire place. Everyone froze in his or her seat. I could sense how wrong the interruption was, but what was I to do?

In a split second the Spirit of the Lord came upon me with the answer. I was not to rise up and correct her. The Spirit said, *Just sit down.*

There I was in the middle of the platform—no chair, no bench, nothing. So I sat down on the floor. Then I looked up and said, "Lady, is your pastor here?"

The effect of these two actions showed that I had taken a lower place and that she had no pastoral covering.

Then I looked at everyone else and said, "If you agree with the message tonight, run down here right now and repent before God."

Almost everybody but the woman rushed down and filled the front of the church, and the power of God swept over those broken, praying people, including many pastors. It turned out to be a very powerful night.

That woman may have felt threatened in the same way that the people in Jesus' day did. He went right for the problem, which shocked them. They wanted their Messiah to go after Rome, in which case they would have crowned Him King and loved Him. But He went after *them,* as though they were the problem, not Rome! He was really saying, "God loves Rome and wants to touch Rome through you, but you won't let Him. So God is going to use Rome to destroy you."

It shocked them. They could not handle it—but what He said came to pass. And if it is true today as well—and I believe it is—then the present religious system must fall into the same category as every religious system that has ever stopped a move of God.

In Israel I saw a beautiful model of Herod's Temple. I had not known it was so large and magnificent. So for Jesus to say, "This is all going to crumble, and in three days I'm going to raise up something else," was absurd and fantastic to them. They could not fathom such a major change.

Good news is coming to the nations, and it will come through a new temple. A new capstone is being laid in our generation—fresh, alive, free of the old religious system that is full of corruption and love of money and people who do not want to be bothered by God. But something has to give way to make a place for this new temple.

When the Kingdom of God is at hand, Kingdom things happen. Jesus said, "If I drive out demons by the finger of God, then the kingdom of God has come to you" (Luke 11:20). The fact that people are getting free today is a sign of the Kingdom. Every pastor who repents and every church that turns is a sign of the Kingdom coming nearer to us. It is a great day and a terrible day. Kingdom things are on the increase, but the current religious opposition must crumble.

Let's be hungry and thirsty and eager for the corruption to fall and the Kingdom to come.

What Was Wrong with Ishmael?

> Hagar bore Abram a son, and Abram gave the name Ishmael to the son she had borne. Abram was eighty-six years old when Hagar bore him Ishmael.
>
> Genesis 16:15–16

In the Old Testament we see a poignant story that proves the same point: When God is bringing something new, the old, worldly system must get out of the way.

God had promised Abraham a son through whom all the nations of the world would be blessed. You would think that when Ishmael was born, God might have used him to fulfill His promise. In fact, Abraham said, "If only Ishmael might live under your blessing!" (Genesis 17:18). But Ishmael was not the one.

You can feel the strain in the story because Abraham loved Ishmael, yet this firstborn son through Hagar was not the one to bless the world. I can hear Abraham asking, "What's wrong with Ishmael? He came from me. He's my son. You promised me a son. Can't You bless him?" The answer from God was, "No." Ishmael, though loved of Abraham and of God, was not the son to carry the promise.

What was wrong with Ishmael? Wouldn't he do? Wasn't he a son of Abraham?

Yes, but Ishmael was born in the power of the flesh, not the power of the Spirit. In Galatians 4:29 Paul says, "At that time the son born in the ordinary way persecuted the son born by the power of the Spirit. It is the same now." That simple statement describes the whole situation. God gives His greatest promises to people and nations and organizations and churches born of the Spirit. The Bible says that Abraham's body at the time of the birth of Isaac, his son through his elderly wife, Sarah, "was as good as dead" (Romans 4:19). God waited for the impossible situation, when Abraham's body and Sarah's womb were as good as dead, to bring forth Isaac, who was essentially born from the dead.

I feel the same strain in the Church today, much of which we have built in the power of the flesh. People say, "What's wrong with my church? Why can't God work through what we already have?" Perhaps because although it may be a good church, it is not the one promised to Jesus.

In Ephesians 5:25–27 we learn that Jesus gave Himself up to win a holy, radiant bride without stain, wrinkle or blemish. What He has today, however, is a divided, apathetic, halfhearted, worldly, backslidden, backstabbing, lukewarm bunch of people. Today's Church was born in the ordinary way. Tomorrow's will be born of the Spirit and will be the Church of the promise.

I am not saying there is no good in today's Church. Hagar and Ishmael, the son according to the flesh, experienced God's compassion in the desert when He came to their rescue. But that did not change the fact that Ishmael was not the son God had promised. He was a son, but not the right one.

What makes a son the right one? The pattern I see in the Bible is that God nurtures His promises in dead situations, when there is no help apart from divine intervention. Jesus was born out of a grave. He was not sort of dead; He was absolutely dead, and He had to come back to life. Life had to come from death—the promised Messiah by the power of the Spirit.

And what about us, the followers of Christ? The Bible says, "When you were dead in your sins and in the uncircumcision of your sinful nature, God made you alive with Christ" (Colossians 2:13).

What is wrong with the modern-day Church? Despite many good elements in the Church today, these do not necessarily make her what God has promised. The Church in her present-day condition will never inherit the promise of God, because many of our programs and ideas, which we dreamed up to keep people interested and entertained and to help them through times of struggle, were born in the ordinary way. In some churches, in fact, these programs and ideas are essentially the same ones corporations and governments use. They deal with divorce; we deal with divorce. They deal with drugs; we deal with drugs. They deal with depression; we deal with depression. Such programs and ideas are not necessarily bad, but they are ordinary institutions not born of the Spirit of God. And those churches, for all they have done, will never be the Church of the promise.

I had some questions about this clear back in 1984 when God impressed on me to pioneer Smithton Community Church.

Lord, I thought, *do we really need another church?*

Someone starts a new church that is basically like every other church, and he or she takes over as the head. Each new church that comes along has a particular form of music. Most try to evangelize and help the hurting. But I did not want to follow the crowd and head another church doing the same things. Then I began to realize God was looking for a different kind of church—one centered exclusively on Him. He did not need another congregation full of wandering, wavering believers trying to hang on until Jesus returned.

In many churches commitment to Jesus is never mentioned. People drift in and out as they please. It is standard fare to put job and sports and sleep and money first. But God wants to raise up a people who will seek His Kingdom first, a people whose only desire is to serve Him with their whole hearts.

I knew what Jesus was calling for, but where were the people to follow His plan? Jesus wants churches through which He can show His power and glory. But first the people must prove themselves in loyalty and faithfulness with a single eye and a single mind.

I sensed God calling me to raise up a different kind of people who wanted nothing more than to be in the presence of God and to know His glory. What a battle it has been! Through the years people came and left. Some did pretty well, and then for some reason faded back to the middle of the road. Others started out knowing the will of God for their lives, but somehow, like Judas, allowed Satan to enter their hearts, and then they turned ugly on the inside.

Happily there were some who came and stayed and believed and never wavered. These are the ones for whom God opened heaven on March 24, 1996, after twelve years of labor in faith and love. They have seen a church born out of a promise.

Although the Holy Spirit must do the work, we must separate ourselves to Him and to His work alone. Anything else becomes just another church born in the ordinary way.

The Radiant Church to Come

The inbreaking Kingdom is giving birth to a different kind of church. It is unpredictable, exciting. It is a lot of work. It is spontaneous. When people meet, things happen that can come only from God. Suddenly prayer gets results. People break away from lifelong habits and a flood of love is released in their hearts.

The way God is moving in parts of the Church today makes it hard to give any human being glory. This is a revival people did not plan. There is nothing ordinary about it. It was born out of the power of God.

I want to be involved in something that human beings cannot create, sustain or even fully understand—and that is what the inbreaking Kingdom is. It calls us out of our graves and unwraps us from our graveclothes and sends us back into the world alive. What was wrong with Ishmael? His birth was not a supernatural work of the Spirit of God. What is wrong with the Church? She is not the one promised to Jesus. We will be a Church not born in the corporate headquarters but like the impossible promise given Abraham by the Spirit of God.

The Church promised Jesus will not lead a double life, and she will not be full of guilt because she is having a secret love affair with the world. Jesus was promised a radiant, glorious bride, blameless and holy, without spot or wrinkle. He does not have that bride yet—but He will.

3

A Change of Hands

"But the tenants said to one another, 'This is the heir. Come, let's kill him, and the inheritance will be ours.' So they took him and killed him, and threw him out of the vineyard. What then will the owner of the vineyard do? He will come and kill those tenants and give the vineyard to others."

Mark 12:7–9

THE revival God has brought to parts of the Church has initiated great cleansing and personal repentance. Many hearts that were hard have grown tender, and people no one expected to turn to God have become faithful followers. But the Almighty is not finished with us. He is taking us beyond what we know as revival to a new place of power and intimacy with Him. He is looking for thirsty people—those whose longing for Him is never quenched, who expect Him to do unpredictable, wonderful things and who are willing to pay the cost, whatever it may be.

Sadly, though, as we make the transition to the new place God has for us, some people will not make it.

They will find that the vineyard has changed hands and God's Kingdom resources have been given to others, as happened in the parable in Mark's gospel. The parable of the vineyard speaks to us today by foretelling what will happen as this present move of God unfolds, and I want to focus in this chapter on its content.

Jesus did not tell stories just for their entertainment value; He told them because they were attractive packages in which to convey something true about His Kingdom or about His listeners, and often the listeners were able to recognize themselves in the stories. In Mark 12:12, for example, the Pharisees "looked for a way to arrest him because they knew he had spoken the parable against them."

We Christians are fond of gloating over the Pharisees' failures, but we ought to make sure we do not fall into the same trap of pride that snapped shut on them. Some of us are so prideful that we cannot find ourselves in the Bible anymore. We are blind to the weaknesses and problems Jesus talked about. We are more than happy to watch Him give it to the Pharisees, but we refuse to let the same words penetrate and search our own hearts. In truth most of us would find a lot of Pharisaism in ourselves if we stopped treating the Scriptures as a spectator sport and took Jesus' words seriously.

A Parable about Us

As we look at what the parable in Mark 12 involves, a few truths jump out immediately. The owner of the vineyard is obviously God. The ones sent to collect the fruit are the servants and prophets of God. The son is Jesus. But who are the tenants?

The quick answer is, "The tenants are the Jews because they killed Jesus." That sounds logical but it is not accurate. Jesus is not talking about all Jews. All the apostles were Jewish. Every evangelist in the early days was Jewish. God is not pointing a finger at the Jews; He is pointing to anyone with a condition of the heart leading him or her to kill His servants and prophets. In Jesus' day God took the vineyard from one group of Jewish people whom He had called and gave it to another group of Jewish people who continued to walk with God.

In the broader sense this parable is about people who belong to a corrupt religious system that refuses to accept God's word through His servants and that does not bear fruit. Certainly the Pharisees listening to Jesus had never killed any prophets, yet they knew He was talking about them because they were financing and benefiting from a religious system that had silenced many prophets. They may not have committed the crimes; they may not have preached the sermons that deceived. But they were part of a system that did that and more, and they were unwilling to relinquish their vested interest in that system's survival.

Fast forward two thousand years, and you find a similar system posing in many places as the Church. It may or may not characterize your local congregation, but we have all encountered the religious system that says things like, "The power of God ended with the apostles," and, "God doesn't work that way anymore." Countless thousands of men and women are enmeshed in this ungodly system. They may not actually have done any of the things that brought us to this point of desperation. Many are probably genuinely eager and hungry for God. But even though they do not preach the sermons or promote the false teachings, they have financed, cultivated and benefited from a system that is actually resisting, rather than advancing, God's Kingdom.

That is what the parable in Mark 12 is about. It is not aimed just at the Pharisees; it is aimed at you and me.

What is the progression that brings the tenants to a point of killing the owner's son? In the story the owner sends his servants to collect fruit from the vineyard. This is a reasonable expectation. They would have made an agreement ahead of time that a certain percentage of the fruit would belong to the owner.

Anyone who makes a commitment to Christ does the same thing. God says, in His unfathomable grace, "I am going to let you work in My vineyard. I am going to save you. I am going to straighten out your life, and I want you to work for Me and produce good fruit." We agree, saying, "I want to produce good fruit. Use me, Lord. Send me. I'll go, I'll be, I'll sing, I'll preach." But when it comes time actually to work for Him, many bow out: "I'm pretty busy. I've got a lot of pressure on me right now. I'm in the mood to stay home tonight and watch TV and relax a little bit."

When the owner's servants come to collect what is rightfully his, then, they meet up with more than murder and brutality. They meet with greed and the love of things, which makes these workers treacherous. Instead of abiding by the original contract, they redraw the lines. "Hey, we can have everything," they reason. "We don't have to give anything away, and we don't have to serve him."

The owner finally sends his only son, which in the Kingdom of God is the same as sending Himself. As Jesus tells the story, we want to warn Him not to go. After all, they are going to kill Him. But He does, and they do.

Then Jesus poses this question: "What then will the owner of the vineyard do?" (verse 9). The answer is twofold. First, He will kill the selfish tenants. That fits the logical plot line, doesn't it? And second, He will give the vineyard to others.

Who Will Be Faithful?

I am convinced that when this story plays itself out in reality in our day, the twofold response may come in a different order. That is, the first result will not be that people keel over and die. I think they will lose the vineyard first. Isn't that what happened to Adam? He sinned against God but did not fall over dead. He got to live—but he lived outside the vineyard, the Garden of Eden. The same thing happened to the Pharisees. They did not die right after Jesus was crucified. It was forty years before Jerusalem was destroyed, and some of the Pharisees died at the hands of the Romans. Probably most of the Pharisees from Jesus' day were dead from natural causes already. But the vineyard had long since changed hands. God's Kingdom had passed right on by.

We must understand that the principles in these parables apply to us just as much as they did to the Pharisees. The innate wickedness of the human heart has not changed. Furthermore God would not put something useless in the Bible for us to read. This is not about history; it is about us. The Bible is a revelation of who we are, shown through the prism of the lives of others.

In His pattern God is saying that it is necessary at certain times in history to wrest the Kingdom out of the hands of the corrupt and put it into the hands of the faithful. This is an everlasting principle. In Jesus' day there had to be a change of hands, or the Kingdom would have produced no more fruit, since it was in the care of treacherous and dangerous men. They had to be removed, then, and the vineyard given to another group—an outcast group, who we know proved more faithful.

Today a change of hands is taking place from those who have dealt selfishly with the things of God to those who will be trustworthy. I do not know how God decides the moment at which to divest certain people and institutions of His Kingdom resources and invest them in others, but I am sure it has a lot to do with conditions of the heart that we cannot see. I know that God's mercy and patience with men and women are great, and that He does nothing rashly.

One of the heartbreaks of being a pastor for many years is watching the "could-have-beens" and the "should-have-beens." These are the people whom God gave an equal opportunity to be part of the coming Kingdom, but who quit the race. I can think of dozens who have passed through Smithton Community Church who should be here to participate in this move of God.

One particular couple I believe God hand-picked for such an hour as this had potential but allowed pride and arrogance to enter their hearts. They began to think they could have a separate ministry within the church without the need of a pastor. They also felt they had a unique anointing, and that they had arrived where God wanted them to be. This couple became more defiant and critical until their relationship with the church collapsed. God moved them out and gave their ministry to someone else. That couple could and should have been part of a revival that is touching the world, but their motives were impure. God moved them out and took their section of the vineyard away.

When the Lord decides it is time for a change of hands, we can know it is the right time. God wants the Kingdom to flourish. Right now, all over the world, people are being tested—not to see who is the most talented or holy, but to see who is the most faithful and humble. This move of God has shed great light on what resides in the hearts of some who name the name of Christ: divisiveness, criticism, treachery, laziness, lying, hypocrisy. There are people in key positions throughout the church world—many of whom control the money or the spiritual climate—who do not want a move of God because it challenges the system that supports them.

I remember meeting a godly woman who had served God for many years and now held a prestigious position in her denomination. Yet with all her knowledge and years of service, she was adamantly opposed to the present-day revival. It made no sense because she had seen the power of God in her life in mighty ways. Why was she not rejoicing with others at what God was doing? The answer seemed to be that in order to accept a fresh move of God, one has to admit that such a move is needed. In fact, this woman had been swept into her position in just such a move of God, but she had grown comfortable there and did not want to change. Yielding to a new move of God was like having the rug pulled out from under her. Rather than accept it humbly, she fought back with criticism and judgment, defending the system she was part of.

That system, in large part, so opposes the fresh inbreaking of the Kingdom today that the situation resembles the biblical pattern. But what a day to be alive and in love with God! He is saying to the most unlikely people, "Here, do you want this? I've got to give it to somebody, because if I don't, the Kingdom will come to a close. The vineyard is not producing. There is no fruit. The current owners are stealing, robbing and feeding themselves. It's got to change hands, and I'd like to offer it to you."

A human being could not hear words more precious or profound.

One night during the prayer time in one of our revival services, a pastor came up to the front and told me he needed prayer for what was taking place at his church. He looked as if someone had beaten him and thrown him into the street. He had lost control of his church to a group that did not want a move of God.

As I prayed for him, I began to feel as though God were stirring a boiling pot. I sensed God's hand moving faster, stirring the pot as it simmered hotter and hotter. This broken man was transformed before my eyes. Sweat broke out on his forehead; pressure was building up inside of him. When the water came to a full boil, the steam suddenly blew out like a whistle on a tea kettle, and he began shouting, "Yes! Yes! Yes!" His arms shot up into the air, his fists clenched. I did not know what the "yes" meant to him or to God, but I saw before me a man full of faith, determination and authority.

I learned later that he went back to his church and walked in as if he had been anointed by Samuel. As he spoke with confidence and fire, the hearts of the rebellious people began to break. Because of their strong repentance, God granted that congregation a dramatic transformation of heart that prevented a tragic change of hands.

Working for God

Every person goes through situations intended to help pry them away from their love of the world and prepare them to receive a new measure of God's Kingdom. My father's death was like that for me; it is one of the experiences that has had the most impact on my life. I was sixteen years old at the time, but the event still affects me. I realized that life can end, and what do you really have to show for it?

The Bible contains many parables that say, in essence, "Make the most of your time. Don't waste it. Lay up for yourselves treasures in heaven." At sixteen I started taking those messages seriously. I also began to notice many people who do not live with a sense that life can end. My father's death opened me more to working for God because I realized that, eternally speaking, the moments I did *not* do so would not count for much.

Just as this is true individually, so corporately we must accept the reality of what it means to open our hearts to the work God wants to do. Otherwise the Church will continue to multiply lukewarm and halfhearted people, the depressed, the oppressed and the suicidal. We see the pattern of God. Those who cultivate, finance, keep alive or promote a corrupt religious system that bears no fruit will be cut off, cut down, thrown into the fire, cast away, thrown out or replaced.

Some people have a hard time believing God will do that, but look at this simple statement from Jesus:

> "You are the salt of the earth. But if the salt loses its salti-ness, how can it be made salty again? It is no longer good for anything, except to be thrown out and trampled by men."
>
> Matthew 5:13

Every Christian likes to think he or she is the salt of the earth, but we tend to leave off the part about what happens if the salt loses its saltiness. Again it is a pattern. You can be the salt. God will make you the salt. He *wants* you to be the salt. But if you squander this identity and lose your saltiness, you are good only to be thrown out and trampled by men.

That is where we live today. God is testing the salt for saltiness. He is checking the lamps for light. He is looking over the tenants who have worked the vineyard.

Some believe the current religious system can go on unaltered, untouched and unthreatened. I am saying the opposite. God is going to make His move, taking the vineyard from one group and giving it to another—unless our hearts change.

Those of us who have been Christians for many years must be careful in these days to examine ourselves. Many of us are lukewarm without knowing we are lukewarm. Many more have been lulled into complacency. What is lacking in many churches today is fear of the Owner of the vineyard. Some of us just want to be entertained and to have fun; we have no intention of respecting the wishes of His Son when He shows up. It is easy for us to forget that God still sends His Son to the Church. Consider Revelation 3:20:

> "Here I am! I stand at the door and knock. If anyone hears my voice and opens the door, I will come in and eat with him, and he with me."

I have heard this passage preached out of context more than any other. In order to make it not apply to us, we turn it into an evangelistic statement. But Jesus is not addressing this message to the unsaved. He is standing and knocking on the door of the Church, and the Church will not let Him in. Many have been lulled into complacency and no longer see that they are dancing on the edge of a cliff.

Is it possible that pride and love of power were worse in the Temple in Jesus' day than in churches now? Is it possible that our corruption is not as bad as the corruption of the Jewish leaders who crucified Jesus? Is it possible that they loved money more than we do?

I cannot imagine it. Many in the Church are just as corrupt and in love with the things of the world as the leaders in the first century. It is not unthinkable. The Bible is full of stories that show the people of God becoming corrupt in their desires. And time after time, God takes from those who are proud and self-assured and gives to those who are humble and lowly in heart.

Many of the present tenants work for the good of denominations and organizations; the new tenants will work only for the good of the Owner. The present tenants have become conspirators to maintain a religious status quo; the new tenants will allow Jesus to lead wherever and however He wants. The present tenants have allowed their pure devotion to become tainted with greed; the new tenants will not seek their own gain at all. The present tenants extinguish any appearance of God; the new tenants will live in continual revival until Jesus comes.

God still sends His Son to churches, movements, youth groups, denominations and individuals. He is still saying the same thing as the owner of the vineyard in Jesus' parable: "Perhaps this time I will find people who will respect and receive My Son." He is determined, before the season ends, that the vineyard produce fruit. Thus He is giving it over to new tenants—and if He finds in you a willing heart, you can be one of them.

Part 2

Where Are We Now?

A Powerless God

> Although they claimed to be wise, they became fools and exchanged the glory of the immortal God for images made to look like mortal man and birds and animals and reptiles. Therefore God gave them over in the sinful desires of their hearts to sexual impurity for the degrading of their bodies with one another. . . . Furthermore, since they did not think it worthwhile to retain the knowledge of God, he gave them over to a depraved mind, to do what ought not to be done. They have become filled with every kind of wickedness, evil, greed and depravity. They are full of envy, murder, strife, deceit and malice. They are gossips, slanderers, God-haters, insolent, arrogant and boastful; they invent ways of doing evil; they disobey their parents; they are senseless, faithless, heartless, ruthless.
>
> Romans 1:22–24, 28–31

HOW I used to long for the glory of God to come into our services! Then, in the first few services after revival struck, God's presence came to us in a way that I had never experienced. We had had good services, but now something was different. At certain times the glory came drifting in without warning. God's presence would become thick and almost tangible. Many times

I would look up and see into the throne room of God. (Perhaps people wondered what I could possibly be staring at for such a long time!)

At times I can still see Jesus seated on His mighty throne. At very rare times, maybe when the praise of the people sounds like thunder, Jesus will slowly stand up as if joining in. He becomes so real that I feel I can almost reach out and touch Him. During such times the invisible becomes more real to me than the visible, the immortal than the mortal, the permanent than the temporary. It is like living in a dream, when the shackles of time break away and my world begins to float on a cloud of God's presence.

How inconceivable, then, that the people of God, who had "the glory of the immortal God" (Romans 1:23), exchanged it for something else! How could anyone exchange God's glory for something else? It is as though the Kingdom is on full throttle and there is nothing more to think about.

As we recognize the power behind God's Kingdom as it comes, we must also understand the scene today into which the Kingdom is breaking, particularly as it relates to our perception of God. To help us discern what is happening, let's look back at Jesus and His ministry.

In Israel the religious Jews had a form of godliness but no power. They had legalism and conformity and condemnation but no freedom. Few taught with real authority, and the so-called men of God (Jesus called them children of the devil) were involved in religion for their own gain.

Similarly today we find a Church with little power and a lot of people working for their own profit. We do not see the kind of power and authority in which Jesus and His disciples operated. Not many of us who attend church, for example, often see someone being delivered from demonic oppression or from lifelong bondage to sin. Seldom do we see sick people get healed or experience the presence of God so powerfully that the entire congregation falls prostrate for a long time in reverence and worship. It is not even common to see those in total rebellion get turned around to become radical servants of Jesus.

Revival has changed this, of course. It is by no means rare these days to see the glory of God come into worship services, including at Smithton Community Church—but it was not always this way. This move of God is as new to me as to anybody, and it yields many results I do not understand. I have seen grown men fall out of their chairs under conviction during the preaching of God's Word. I have seen hundreds collapse in seeming agony over their own spiritual condition as the presence of God collides with their humanity. It is like something out of the history books detailing the great revivals of the past, including the Great Awakening, the Cane Ridge revival and the Welsh revival.

We find ourselves in a unique time on God's calendar— a time of the release of His power and anointing to people who never expected it; a time of grace and judgment; a time of legitimate revival that strikes at the very core of who and what we are.

A Powerless Church

But the power of God these days is confined to a handful of churches. As much as I love the Church and her people, I realize that most of us experience a devastating lack of power.

Some churches I visit do not pretend to know anything about the power of God, which can work two ways. It makes them either more skeptical when God begins to move during a service, or more open. Other churches profess the power of God but have nothing to bear out their claims. I cannot count the number of times I have seen a pastor walk to the pulpit after congregational praise and worship and say, "God is here tonight," or, "I can feel the power of God all over this place," when there is no evidence of God's power in that place, and people leave with the same sin and selfishness they came in with. When we say things like this, we are trying to reduce God's power to something we understand.

How futile our efforts have become when a cheerleading pastor claims that revival has come to a dull and lifeless congregation, yet the teens sit in a worldly stupor, children play with their toys and color on the bulletin and the adults are preoccupied with how soon the service will end and whom they will talk with afterward. The Holy Spirit is grieved and driven away by our lackluster desire for God, even as we sing, "Oh, how I love Jesus!"

God's power is so radically beyond our comprehension that to try to describe it with words on a page is almost laughable. This is the God who manufactured every bit of matter in the universe out of nothing—billions of galaxies containing trillions of stars, comets, black holes, planets, moons, asteroids and celestial bodies we have not even begun to discover. This God measures in numbers so great that "trillions" looks like child's play. This God holds the universe in place with a single word and commands thousands of angels, whose presence holds the heavens in its thrall and who will captivate our attention for eternity. This God created every insect, animal and plant that science has ever discovered. He breathed life into all living things and arranged the natural world in all its intricacy, down to the tiniest particle.

Imagine what would happen if God in all His power visited your church and you began to see what a charade we are making of the worship of the living God, in a day when church is considered one of the most boring places on the planet! There is so much of Him we have not experienced, and so much He wants us to do as His children, that even the greatest glories of the present revival only hint at what believers will see in the future.

One thing is certain: Where God's power is present, lives are changed. Where God's power is present, there is no cycle of backsliding and recommitment, as we see in many of our churches today. Frankly, what the Church today calls power is a sad and sickly thing compared to what God calls power. Often we say we want more of God, but our actions betray our lack of commitment. Some of us are in love with our own power or position. Splits, self-love, gossip and backbiting tear at the fabric of the Church. We are in large part stuck in a backslidden, lukewarm, hypocritical, powerless system that can be reversed only by complete reformation.

This reformation is now under way, and there are only two sides: those who accept God for who He is, power and all, and those who will not. This crisis taking place within the Church does not involve sinners; it involves professing believers.

Saying Yes to God . . .

For Christians who welcome the power of God, these are the most wonderful days of their lives.

One night a pastor named Todd walked into a Smithton service. He had been baptized in the Holy Spirit and had begun to preach with new fire, both of which caused problems in the church he was pastoring. Eventually his denomination asked him to leave. Now, broken and hurting, his ministry cut short, he began coming to Smithton.

During the time of praise one evening, the Spirit of the Lord prompted me to make a quick charge down the aisle, near to where Todd was sitting. I did so not knowing what to expect, nor had I ever met or spoken to Todd. I had not gotten within five feet of him when I thrust forward my hand, feeling as if a sword were in it. I did not actually touch this man, but he flew back, hit the floor and remained there in a fetal position for hours.

From my point of view, that was the end of the incident. But Todd told us later he had been freed from the pain inflicted by losing his pastorate. Soon he became a member of our church and got active on one of our ministry teams.

Not long afterward he had yet another shocking experience. He was with the team ministering to a congregation in Wichita Falls, Texas, and he and some friends were leaving someone's home during a thunderstorm. Todd grabbed an umbrella and headed for the car when a blinding bolt of lightning and a massive explosion shook the ground. Todd was struck by lightning. The umbrella flew out of his hands and he was knocked off his feet. To his friends' amazement, however, he jumped up and ran into the house. Doctors found nothing wrong with him except an unusual red streak across his chest.

His story made the paper and the television news. "I've been struck by lightning from the sky," Todd told them, "and was able to get up after a few seconds. But when Pastor Steve Gray prayed for me, I was struck by the lightning of God and was unable to get up for hours!"

Some time later Todd took a church in Missouri and is pastoring once again. He said yes to the power of God, who continued to direct his steps and protect him. Todd went through despair, losing both his church and his denomination, but he allowed God in, and now testifies that there is no other way to live.

. . . Or Staying in Control?

Many of us, by contrast, are afraid of a God who comes down from heaven and interferes with our daily routine. We prefer a powerless God who leaves us alone now but gives us eternal life after we die. Instead of divine power, we tend to choose programs, church politics and powerless religion that bear scarcely any resemblance to the group of believers on whom Jesus sent His Spirit in the book of Acts.

Oh, we may not have written it on a prayer request card or asked for it in our private devotions, but we request it with our actions and thoughts: "Be a God who doesn't demand our effort and who won't lay claim to our lives. Give us the moving of the Spirit, but in a tightly controlled framework so we won't make anyone nervous and so we can go home early."

It is common for Christians today to suggest that America needs to return to the spiritual roots of our founding fathers. Many do not realize, however, that many of those men were deists—that is, they believed God created the earth but that He left it alone to run its course, and left humans to fend for themselves with the wisdom He gave them. I have had to fight the impulse in my own life to treat God as an absent father, a faceless deity, the "man upstairs."

Rather than go back to the faith of America's founding fathers, then, I would rather go back much further—to the days of the New Testament, where prophets and apostles laid the foundation for the Church. If we are going to look back, why not look to what Jesus Himself established?

It grieves me to think we have gotten so far from God that when He does something unusual, like break through in a tiny town in Missouri, it is a major event. Christians marvel at the slightest show of power—power that was normal for believers in the book of Acts! Many of us have allowed our concept of power to be reduced to the point of ineffectiveness. We talk about miracles, wonders and revival, but we go only halfway. We want a powerful revival that leaves us alone; a church where things happen during the service but from which our home lives can remain distinct. We want lively worship and a few healings sprinkled throughout the year, but nothing that threatens our "me" time. We call for revival in the sanctuary but get queasy when God calls us to a more strenuous commitment.

Some Christians who say they love revival can be just as selfish as those who oppose it, because they want a God who lets them run the show. The same spirit of control is at work in both groups. The one wants revival but with an expiration date. They want enough of God to know He loves them, but not enough to remind them that "whoever finds his life will lose it, and whoever loses his life for my sake will find it" (Matthew 10:39).

We have grown comfortable with a powerless god, but we are paying for it. Preachers preach, "All is well," but all is not well. Any pastor can tell sad stories coming out of our churches: divorce, secret sins, pride, pornography, suicide. Everything afflicting society also afflicts even the biggest and best churches. Who do we think we are? How can we presume to stand back and say, "God, bring revival to the world," when we have so much of the world in our churches? How can we invoke the name of the Lord when many pulpits across America have become platforms for the preaching of a God of limited power, a God of used-to-be power?

If you believe in a powerful God these days, even some Christians will call you weak-minded and immature. We want a forgettable message from God and we are sliding closer and closer to outright apostasy. However abrupt that assessment may seem, I believe it is largely the state we find ourselves in.

A Giving-In and a Giving God

It is a profound mistake to imagine a God who will never reject us. Scripture is clear about this: "If we endure, we will also reign with him. If we disown him, he will also disown us" (2 Timothy 2:12). When the Kingdom comes and we refuse it, we lose it. The Kingdom does not stop, but it will pass us by if we let it.

Someone might point to the many promises Jesus made to His disciples—that He would never leave or forsake them, that He would be with them always, even until the end of the age. Certainly that applies to any disciple of Christ. But if we look at the pattern of the original twelve disciples, we see that they left everything and gave up their very lives for the Gospel. Do the same promises apply to half-committed Christians or to a backsliding Church?

That, I believe, is beyond the realm of credibility. Our ears are so attuned to hearing about God's love and mercy that we hardly recognize the God Paul wrote about in Romans 1:21, 24:

> For although they knew God, they neither glorified him as God nor gave thanks to him, but their thinking became futile and their foolish hearts were darkened. . . . Therefore God gave them over in the sinful desires of their hearts to sexual impurity for the degrading of their bodies with one another.

Paul was not talking about ignorant people who did not know God. The people he was discussing knew God, but in spite of their knowledge made foolish decisions against Him. This passage further illustrates how God behaves toward those who persist in their sinful desires, sexual or otherwise.

Our Father is very interested in our desires. He looks to our hearts to see what we long to be doing. If God did not listen to our desires, wouldn't prayer be useless? Nor is He one to make idle threats; He is a God of His promises, for better or worse. Thus He gave those people who knew God over to the things they really wanted. He is not only a giving God, but a giving-in God.

Today He has in large part given the Church over to powerless religion, because that is what so many of us really want. When we demand things long enough, He gives them to us, just as He gave Israel the king they clamored for, just as He gave the people Paul wrote about in Romans "over in the sinful desires of their hearts." Although they had evidence of God's hand at work, they denied Him. They knew of God's glory but chose not to allow Him in, so the giving-in God gave them over to what they wanted: a deity who did not interfere in their lives.

Psalm 34:8 says, "Taste and see that the Lord is good." The modern message, if it holds any conviction at all, is often spoken as though the listener has never tasted of the Lord. But it is rare to find anyone in this country who has never heard of Jesus. Go to any bar, any drug-infested neighborhood, and people know about Jesus. Not only that, but they know a lot about Him. The average person can tell the story of His birth, the angels, the manger, the miracles, His death on a cross and His resurrection from the dead. They may not have the theology, but they have the facts.

People are not ignorant of the Son of God; they have decided they want something else. It is not that we have not tasted of God, but that we have no taste for God.

Since the beginning of time, if human beings know the facts, they are accountable. How did God respond to

Adam and Eve when they sinned? Did He hand out tracts or plead with them to reconsider their foolish ways? No, He cast them away from the Garden and His presence. It was more than the death sentence to their bodies; it was the death sentence to their intimacy with their Creator.

Millions are walking around enslaved to their sinful condition because of that one decision. God gave in. He respects the decisions of the men and women He fashioned with His own hands.

Christians deceive themselves into thinking they have God's presence because they have knowledge of Him. But God's presence and the knowledge of God are two different things. Adam and Eve in the Garden ate from the tree of the knowledge of good and evil, but they lost the presence of God. They still knew about God, but they did not have Him in the same intimate way.

The knowledge of God can be a dangerous thing, as the above passage from Romans indicates, because the knowledge of God makes us responsible for how we respond. Many in the Church are skewed almost completely to the side of knowing about God, while they rarely experience His presence.

Of the thousands of people each year whom I pray for, I am thankful for those who are mightily and powerfully touched, but I also see that some have no response left for God. Multitudes of churchgoers have given themselves over to the world to such a degree that they have no room left for God's presence. They cannot respond to Him. They hide this disability with weak excuses like "I wasn't brought up that way" or "I'm not an emotional person." Yet these same people can respond with tears to a sports event or a make-believe movie with pretend people. A stony-faced pew-warmer can respond emotionally to a sexual act on the silver screen but have no feeling for the living God of the universe.

The people about whom Paul wrote worshiped created things and devalued the glory of God to a level that they could understand and control. In America we worship created things, too—cars, money, jobs, careers, vacations, sports, day-planners, videos. To a greater degree than we realize, we are idol-worshipers and lovers of ourselves. We seek wealth, comfort and peace of mind through all different means, and on Sundays many of us play at church.

God hates it. He has in large measure already given us over to our lusts because that is what we have insisted on. Christians do not have a belief problem; we have a control problem. Do we really want the Kingdom to break through so that Jesus becomes Lord and begins to exert His power on the earth? If we do, our lives will no longer be our own.

In the book of Acts God shook the building where the first Christians prayed, showing us how in tune they were with their risen Savior. They were not leading anymore; He was. They became servants and let Him be the Lord, and as a result He stayed involved at every turn of the road.

Today if we got together and prayed and the building shook, it would be very biblical, but many would not come back because they would think the devil did it! Traditional Protestant Christianity dating from Martin Luther's Reformation has attributed many works of power to Satan. God is presented as powerless; Satan is presented as powerful. It is the opinion of many in the church that Satan performs signs and wonders but that God does not. We are quick to point out the devil's handiwork, but any sign of God working becomes a theological controversy, and the Spirit is quenched.

We look at drug addicts and the bondage they are in and know it is the handiwork of Satan. Yet when God transforms a man's heart and he becomes radical for Jesus, we may think he has swung too far the other way. We prefer people in the neutral zone, under the control of neither Satan nor God but under their own control—because we ourselves want to remain in charge.

We resist the power of God as much as we do the power of Satan. When demonic power enters the picture, we have all sorts of solutions to offer—psychology, twelve-step programs, inner healing, counseling, support groups, motivational seminars, uplifting books. These supports let us retain control over the situation. The danger when the Kingdom breaks in is that, in fear, we will deny it is God's power at all, ascribing it either to Satan or to emotional excess.

God is still a giving God, however, and we should be thankful that many believers today—and you may be one of them—have set out to change God's mind; to ask Him to be the powerful God that He is; to see regular manifestations of His power on the earth.

Restoring God's Power

Such a man was the prophet Isaiah. In Isaiah 59 we see a picture of the Church today—powerless, devastated, captive to a godless ruler who made the people of God the laughingstock of the earth. Why had this happened? Israel's history tells the tale, and it can be summed up like this: Israel wanted the world, and God gave it to her. But it did not come the way she expected. Instead of receiving the world's finery, she got a stampeding army of thousands upon thousands of chariots destroying Jerusalem and taking her captive to Babylon. Now the Israelites were slaves to the world they wanted to rule.

The same is true today. If you want the world, you had better be careful. You will try to be king and end up a slave. People today want to head up their organizations, their churches, their denominations. They want to lead the parade, but they end up in shackles because they loved the power of this world. Friendship with the world always ends in slavery because the world is under the control of Satan.

Isaiah looked over the desolate city and reflected that God's people had become slaves to the world, carted off to Babylon. Israel had chosen a powerless god who could not defend her against her own choice. But then Isaiah said these words:

> For Zion's sake I will not keep silent, for Jerusalem's sake I will not remain quiet, till her righteousness shines out like the dawn, her salvation like a blazing torch.
>
> Isaiah 62:1

Why did Isaiah say this? Because even though Israel got what she wanted, she knew God's mind could change, and the prophet made it his goal to work for Israel's restoration. Isaiah set out to change God's mind because God is a giving-in *and* a giving God.

Today people of the same spirit as Isaiah have recognized that the Kingdom is breaking in. They want God to change the course of history so that Christ is no longer mocked in comedy clubs or snorted at among media barons or snubbed by professing Christians. They want the Church to be held in high esteem because the power of God is among us. Like Isaiah these Kingdom warriors will not quit until they see the vision come to pass.

> I have posted watchmen on your walls, O Jerusalem; they will never be silent day or night.
>
> verse 6

Notice that Isaiah's scene is getting broader. It started out with one man, but he has been joined by other watchmen who will not be silent.

Usually watchmen are posted to tell us when the enemy is coming, but in Isaiah's time that would have been ridiculous. The enemy had already come and gone. Nobody was there to be defended. So, why the watchmen? Because another function of watchmen is to sound the alarm when relief is on the way. When the armies of heaven begin to show up, God needs watchmen to proclaim what He is doing, to warn and encourage us that the Kingdom is indeed breaking in.

Many in the Church have been taken captive, but God is gathering His strength because people around the world have made it their ambition to change His mind. God will not be blasphemed in His own house; rebellion against Him will once again be dangerous. Watchmen everywhere are saying, "God is coming!" For now people can whisper and draw pictures and daydream during services, but God is on the way. We can turn churches into entertainment centers where the truth is not preached, but God is coming. The Kingdom is already breaking through. It is disrupting our lives and bringing a new kind of order and authority to the Church. The watchmen on the walls are saying so, thousands of them, and they are not shutting up.

Watch the scene unfold:

> You who call on the LORD . . .
>
> verse 6

It is getting bigger, from Isaiah to watchmen to everyone who calls on the Lord.

> Give yourselves no rest . . .

That is, anyone who will join the revolution for God.

> And give him no rest till he establishes Jerusalem and makes her the praise of the earth.

verse 7

Many in the Church today are captive to Babylon, given over to slavery. But others are realizing that the windows of heaven have opened. More and more Christians are sounding the call of Isaiah. They want a powerful God once again. They want us to see that, if we attempt to maintain control, we settle for a powerless God, but that the Almighty is restoring His power to the Church and that His power is available.

This battle is yours to join. You can make yourself available as a watchman on the wall. I encourage you to sound the alarm with us. Relief is on the way! God is coming with fire to purge and cleanse and deliver us from the slavery we once chose. Let's not wait! Tell your church and your friends that God is on the move again. Give yourself no rest, and give the Lord no rest, until you see His presence restored in your home, church and community.

5

God's House
in Ruins

This is what the LORD Almighty says: "These people say, 'The time has not yet come for the Lord's house to be built.'" Then the word of the Lord came through the prophet Haggai: "Is it a time for you yourselves to be living in your paneled houses, while this house remains a ruin?"

Haggai 1:2–4

It was almost time for me to begin preaching at a church in the Midwest. The pastor and I were sitting in a back room behind the platform before the Sunday evening service, and he was obviously worried. The praise music was booming through the wall and there seemed to be a sizable crowd in the sanctuary. Finally, after fidgeting and moving about nervously for several minutes, he looked at me and said, "Steve, my people love God and many of them want revival, but I just don't know if it's God's time for us yet."

It was not the first time I had heard such a claim, from both pastors and church members around the country. As always it perplexed me. Could it possibly be that the people wanted God desperately, but that God did not want them? Was He biding His time? Leading them on? Did He not love them as much as He claimed to?

After being in such settings and sensing the spirit in the people, it has become clear to me that what they are saying and what God is saying are two different things. Many believers profess to want revival but do not really mean it. There is no evidence that they want revival. Their lives do not reflect a desire to follow Jesus only and forsake all else. So to take the pressure off themselves, they assume it is not the right time.

"You know, Steve," a pastor may say, "I think it's great about revival at Smithton, but I don't know about my church. I think it's just not time yet. My people aren't ready for revival. They would never come to church five days a week the way you do there."

Or people blame God: "Surely if God wanted us to have revival, He would have sent it by now"—assuming that every good thing God wants for us will happen regardless of our own choices.

Building Our Own Houses

Assuming it is not time for revival is not a new attitude. In the book of Haggai we find God's people, just returning from seventy years' captivity in Babylon, saying the same thing. Look again at Haggai 1:2:

> This is what the LORD Almighty says: "These people say, 'The time has not yet come for the LORD's house to be built.'"

You can almost see the smug looks on their faces—as if God had taken some time off and no longer wanted His house, the Temple destroyed by Nebuchadnezzar, to be rebuilt. What did they mean, "It is not time"? They meant, in all honesty, that it was not time because they did not want it to be. They put the work of God on hold because they had better things to do.

Then God asked them, "Is it a time for you yourselves to be living in your paneled houses, while this house remains a ruin?" (verse 4). He mentioned paneled houses because an economic crisis at that point in history made wood scarce. Instead of rebuilding the Temple, as they returned to Judah, the people of God were using any wood they could get for their own houses. They were afraid that if they built God's house first, there would be no wood left for them. They were double-minded and cared less for God's house.

God was saying, "You have it all wrong. It's time for My house to be built, but you don't want to be inconvenienced. It's time once again for the power of God, but you're busy paneling your own houses and doing something else with your time."

What happened because they were building their own houses and leaving God's house a ruin?

> "You expected much, but see, it turned out to be little. What you brought home, I blew away."
>
> verse 9

For the people of Haggai's day as well as ours, the lesson is this: When God's house does not get built, the rest of our lives are affected in the form of diminished returns. God takes away our fruitfulness and our peace—a clear symptom of today's Church.

We are living with disappointment. We expected more of our lives, our marriages, our walks with God. Some of us are so disappointed after we get married that we try to fill the void with children or work or travel or recreation, while our disappointment looms ever larger. Being single did not fill the void; neither does being married or being a father or mother. We try bigger homes, more money, adventures, counseling, psychology, food. We go through life expecting a lot and getting next to nothing because God has diminished our returns. The ground gets harder and harder and crops come at greater cost.

God goes on to say, "I called for a drought . . . on men and cattle, and on the labor of your hands" (verse 11). The Spirit-filled community likes to blame the devil for the lack of harvest, but the Lord says in this passage that He Himself called for it.

Remember, God is talking here to us, the family of believers, not to outsiders. We are the ones going to church but living with holes in our purses (see Hosea 1:6). We want to bind the devil, break generational curses and map our cities for spiritual warfare—and God is drying up our crops.

Why would He do that? Does He want our lives to be unfruitful? No, just the opposite. He wants us to bear the right kind of fruit, and is trying to help us reset our priorities because we have been so busy building our own houses. The heavens are withholding their dew because Christians are busy with other things.

God's way of getting us to notice Him is to withdraw His presence, and eventually we figure it out—"Hey, things aren't going so great here. What's missing?"—and begin to search for God. Many of us are living in disappointment because God is blowing things out of our lives to reveal our utter lack of His presence.

I have known the absence of God, and there is nothing worse than when God seems a million miles away. In the days before revival came to Smithton Community Church, we were a good church on the surface with a faithful group of families, and we could have kept up the act for years, I suppose. We had a full parking lot, a smiling pastor, the right Christian phrases and the right kind of song service. But the divine connection was not there. We began to realize how presumptuous it was to say week after week, "God is in the house," or, "Jesus lives in my heart," when nobody could even tell He was there.

Was it possible that the creative power of the universe could be in us and we did not even know it? Was it possible that the Holy Spirit—the One who raised Christ from the dead—could reside in us and our church and nobody noticed Him? We had claimed His presence for years without demonstrating much evidence. Somehow I had learned to go on in ministry and in life without the presence of God.

When I realized this, I was faced with a choice. I could put on a show, stomp across the stage, wave my Bible in the air and make the people feel as though the noise I made demonstrated the presence of God. Or I could confess to them and to myself that I had lost His presence, and we could go on in some capacity, however limited.

None of us knew that such honesty could turn the heart of God and cause Him to send an outpouring, but that is what happened. (We will talk more about this in later chapters.) When we gave God our time and effort, His Kingdom broke through in a new and profound way that has touched us and others around the world.

Bringing the Glory Back

Today there are more evangelists preaching the Gospel—on television and radio, by satellite, in crusades, in churches, in seminars, in cities and in convention halls—than ever before in the history of mankind. But the ratio of planting to harvesting is embarrassing. We are planting much and harvesting little—not just in our own lives but in the harvest fields of the world. When we look at the work of the Church as a whole, we see how dismal the harvest really is.

Many churches, as we have observed, have lost the presence of God. Worse, many Christians prefer it that way. It is no longer enough to tell believers that they do not have God's presence. Their reaction (I have seen it many times) is, "So what? I've been doing O.K. so far. I'm building my own house. Why do I need God?" It seems we are willing to settle for a limited God rather than seek His presence.

When the word of the Lord came through Haggai, by contrast, it hit the whole nation, not just the priests, and they acted on it. God stirred up the spirits of all the people, even the remnant, and they feared the Lord and obeyed Him. They shut down all other work, went to the mountains, got wood and focused on God's house. And within a month the presence of God returned.

This time He said:

> "'The glory of this present house will be greater than the glory of the former house,' says the LORD Almighty. 'And in this place I will grant peace,' declares the LORD Almighty."
>
> Haggai 2:9

Sometimes we quote this line from Haggai—about the greater glory in the present house—with little reference to what brought about that greater glory. The glory increased not because revival landed like a spaceship out of nowhere and the people happened to be present. Revival came because God gave the returning exiles an opportunity to build His house and they made the choice to do it, even though it cost them time working on their own houses. God knew that if the people tried it, they would not want to go back to their own lives.

In other words, God lays out a cause-and-effect relationship that requires our involvement to make it happen. If we do not work for His house, our fruitfulness will decline drastically; if we build His house, the glory will come back.

What does it mean today to build God's house? Does it mean building physical structures in which to worship? Christians have some of the nicest church buildings on the face of the earth—the best cathedrals, glass structures, stone structures and mega-worship centers, served by parking lots that cover acres of ground. Have we finished most of our work on these buildings? Quite possibly. Then why has His glory not returned? Because our hearts have not changed, as the people's did in Haggai's day. We are not giving ourselves to the true work of building God's house.

When we pray and think continually about Jesus and His Kingdom, we are building God's house. When we gather often with other believers for encouragement and worship; when we make Jesus the center of our homes; when we cultivate the fruit of the Spirit in our lives—then we are building God's house. When we delve deeply into the Bible; when we fall in love with Jesus again; when we give our time, money and effort to the Body of Christ locally—then we are building God's house.

If you want to be part of the advancing Kingdom of God today, you can. I do not know what God's house will look like as it is demonstrated in your life and church, but I know for a fact that the offer is open to literally any congregation, any pastor, any family, any person to have a sovereign, powerful manifestation of God's presence. God wants to pour His Spirit out on us in so great a measure as to make everything in our past seem like wasted time!

The only requirement is a heart that will not waver in devotion to Jesus. Never fall for the idea that "it's not our time yet." That is not the mind of Christ but the mind of man. There is work to do, and it starts with building the temple of the Holy Spirit.

Building the Spiritual House

> Don't you know that you yourselves are God's temple and that God's Spirit lives in you?
>
> 1 Corinthians 3:16

Every person has two houses, the natural (meaning the body) and the spiritual (meaning the inner life with God). Paul said that if our outward house perishes, we know we are being renewed inwardly day by day. Those who build the inward house find that, no matter what the external circumstance, God literally dwells in them. Being filled, infused and saturated with the Holy Spirit day by day is the single greatest human experience!

But too many of us have our priorities wrong. God wants to build the spiritual house and we prefer to build the natural house.

God is interested, certainly, in the natural temple and wants us to take care of what He has entrusted to us. It is hard to believe, however, that He is pleased with our focus on the physical body. Look at the excessive amounts of food we feed it, or the money we spend to decorate it, or the seemingly endless entertainment with which we amuse it. Christians are often no better than the rest of the world in the amount of time we spend obsessed with physical pleasure. Is it any wonder many of us are in danger of missing or even rejecting the inbreaking Kingdom? Jesus said:

"For the pagans run after all these things, and your heavenly Father knows that you need them. But seek first his kingdom and his righteousness, and all these things will be given to you as well."

Matthew 6:32–33

So far we have scarcely listened. In America the natural house gets taken care of first and the spiritual house is left starving. If you could take a picture of today's Christians showing our insides instead of our outsides, many of us would look emaciated. Skinny, skeletal people with broomsticks for legs, swollen stomachs and protruding ribcages, like the photos that come out of impoverished countries when famine hits.

To understand the spiritual drought we are in, try to bring revival and the love of God to your family. Try to get revival to come to your church or city. In many cases it is nearly impossible. People do not realize their spiritual destitution. They have lost their hunger and thirst for God. As usual the problem is not getting new wine but finding new wineskins that will contain what God wants to give. We have in large part forgotten how to build the spiritual house.

But Now, God's Ultimatum

God's temple is in ruins in the midst of material mansions. We are drinking from a stream poisoned by our culture, and it has infected every branch and tributary of our religious system, while God is calling us to build His house. In fact, it is more than an offer; it is an ultimatum:

Don't you know that you yourselves are God's temple and that God's Spirit lives in you? If anyone destroys God's temple, God will destroy him; for God's temple is sacred, and you are that temple.

1 Corinthians 3:16–17

If only Paul had stopped halfway through this passage, we would not have such a problem. We could continue to quote this Scripture to smokers and overweight people, as we love to do, without ever applying the spiritual principle to our own lives, where it belongs. In this passage God is talking about the inner man where the Holy Spirit dwells.

It is the same principle at work as in the book of Haggai. In that day God was destroying the people's fruitfulness, tearing down their work and warning them that if they kept ignoring His house, they would be destroyed. In the same way, if you build your own house, allowing God's house to suffer decay, destruction will come.

This is much more serious than most of us think. Americans see building God's house as an option, not a command. We filter God's words through our culture. "He must mean that we build His house if we have time after soccer practice and piano lessons and grocery shopping and swimming and barbecuing. God can't possibly want me to build His house first. Hasn't He seen my to-do list?" Secretly in our hearts we believe that we will derive no benefit from building God's house.

But we betray our lack of relationship with God when we think of Him as some sort of outdated, heavenly grump. Truly, as we saw in the last chapter, many of us have traded the glory of almighty God for things made by human hands. We do not even know what the glory of God is anymore, or we would respond with fear and obedience to His warning, like the people in Haggai's day.

God is warning us now in this day of the inbreaking Kingdom. God is telling us to stop and assess how we are spending our lives. Our eyes have been blinded by the beautiful houses we are trying to build for ourselves, by the culture we live in and by our own desires. But the consequences of leaving God's house in ruins are serious and imminent. Now is the time to build His house—no matter what people are saying, no matter what the culture believes, no matter how the current religious system responds. He is telling us to make immediate changes, to return to Him so He can bless us. He is a God of today and His heart is full of love toward us. We must not insult Him by weighing Him with the other things taking up our time. The Lord must come first. We must get busy building His house.

If we do, the glory of the present house will indeed be greater than that of the former house. If we do not, God has promised destruction.

Look right now at your own spiritual condition. Are your affections torn, or is Christ at the center of your life? Is working with Him to build the Kingdom the number-one priority in your life?

Focus your thoughts on things above, where Christ is, and He will come in a new and powerful way to your spiritual house. It is not a question of talent, but one of time and effort and priority. When God is your main priority, the Kingdom will break through.

6

Adapted to Demons

"When they came to Jesus, they found the man from whom the demons had gone out, sitting at Jesus' feet, dressed and in his right mind; and they were afraid. Those who had seen it told the people how the demon-possessed man had been cured. Then all the people of the region of the Gerasenes asked Jesus to leave them, because they were overcome with fear. So he got into the boat and left."

Luke 8:35–37

I can see them now—the people standing on the perimeter of the sanctuary, their arms folded over their chests, mouths tight, eyes challenging as they probe and pick apart the service. You can feel their attitude the minute they walk into the building, and it brings a spiritual chill to the air. Sometimes they sit in the front row—a less than pleasant experience for them and me both! They act like the Holy Spirit police, lending their opinions to whatever God does and squelching the Spirit in the name of decorum.

One of the most shocking things to me about the inbreaking Kingdom is this: Not everybody wants it! You might think that the fresh outpouring of mercy and love and power would thrill every Christian to the tips of his toes, but it does not. During times of blessing some people hunker down in their churches like soldiers in a foxhole, hoping to weather the storm, and when revival subsides, they emerge happy from their holes. Others leave their churches altogether, finding different congregations where darkness and a powerless God are still the order of the day and where the Kingdom cannot touch them.

In the last two chapters we looked at several reasons this might be the case. In chapter 4 we saw that many of us do not have a belief problem; we have a control problem. If we allow the Kingdom of God to break through so that Jesus becomes Lord and begins to exert His power on the earth, our lives are no longer our own. Then, in chapter 5, we looked frankly at our widespread apathy and selfishness that causes us to prefer building our own houses rather than God's house. When He is our main priority, His Kingdom will break through.

But there is a third problem. The story of the demonized man in Luke 8 is a picture of where some of us are today in the Body of Christ. Jesus has come down to help us. God is showing us the things in us that do not belong and banishing the darkness from our lives. The Holy Spirit is preparing us for our wedding day. We are in the middle of revival, renewal, refreshing. Yet even as great miracles are happening, the doubts of the past run strong. Fear grips those on the verge of meeting the Master. A crowd mentality overtakes us, and we panic and rush back to what we think is normal life—the familiar, the lifeless, the dead.

The story of the Gerasene demoniac shows the spirit of liberty at war with the spirit of fear, providing a perfect parallel for what we see taking place today.

The Story

The story begins with Jesus getting into a boat and sailing to the region of the Gerasenes. He was met on shore, as if on cue, by a demonized man from the town.

Many translations, such as the New International Version, describe the man as "demon-possessed," but that is a translator's rendering, not the original Greek term. A better rendering of the word is *demonized*. Note that people can be demonized without being possessed. Christians belong to Christ, but by exposing ourselves to various aspects of the world, which is under Satan's influence, we lay ourselves open to torment by demonic entities much bigger and darker than we are. And when we do not devote ourselves entirely to Jesus, a lot of torments can afflict us. We are intended to have one Lover, Jesus, not two.

The description in Luke 8 shows that the Gerasene was very demonized: "For a long time this man had not worn clothes or lived in a house, but had lived in the tombs. . . . Many times [the spirit] had seized him, and though he was chained hand and foot and kept under guard, he had broken his chains and had been driven by the demon into solitary places" (verses 27, 29).

Now the demonized man fell at Jesus' feet and shouted at the top of his voice, "What do you want with me, Jesus, Son of the Most High God? I beg you, don't torture me!" (verse 28).

Demons try to be disruptive because in chaos and confusion they assert some control over a situation. They cause people to shout, writhe or make spectacles of themselves, usually for the purpose of disrupting what God is doing elsewhere. Demons also try to bring an unholy fear into the Body of Christ, and because Christians are so unaccustomed to dealing with demons, the tactic often works. Also, the demon identified Jesus by name as a way of trying to control Him. In the ancient world, in spiritual matters, powers of darkness tried to control people by naming them.

The demoniac declared Jesus "Son of the Most High God" to throw Him off stride, but it did no good; Jesus kept coming at him. The Lord did not always tell demons to reveal their names, so we must not base doctrine on this passage alone, but He did it this time. Jesus threw a question back into the demon's face: "What is your name?" The answer was Legion, "because many demons had gone into him" (verse 30). Then Jesus gave the demons permission to enter the large herd of pigs, which thundered down the hillside into the lake and were drowned.

People came from all around to see this formerly demonized man "sitting at Jesus' feet, dressed and in his right mind." But their response is shocking: "They were afraid" (verse 35).

What they should have feared was a man who lived in the tombs, wore no clothes and could break chains off his arms and legs! That would have scared me. But apparently they could live with that. It was a man at the feet of Jesus in his right mind who scared them.

Afraid of Whom?

Now here is the parallel. A naked man demonized and in chains does not scare us, but the power of God does. Have we, like the Gerasenes, drifted and adapted ourselves to demons to the point of comfort? This man was put in his right mind, and then they were afraid. What is wrong with this picture?

Many troubled people, like the demonized man, come to revivals where the power of God is operating. There they encounter God, and their lives are changed. No longer living among the tombs, they are clothed and put in their right minds, happy and spiritually alive for the first time. But when their friends and neighbors see them in church, sitting at the feet of Jesus, worshiping and adoring Him, raising their hands and shouting praises, they are afraid.

Even when the person testifies, "I was messed up, but Jesus came and saved me, threw the darkness out of my life, and now I want to serve Him, and nothing else matters as much as He does," people shake their heads and say, "Boy, that guy's gone crazy," or, "She's swung too far the other way."

Behind the disgust is fear. I see visitors come into meetings in Smithton, and as soon as the music starts and people jump up and down praising the Lord, the visitors' faces take on a tortured look, as if someone is twisting their arms behind them. I almost wonder why they do not walk out. They remind me of the demonized man when he begged Jesus not to torture him.

We know it was the demons speaking through him, but think of the words coming out of this man's mouth! Who was torturing whom? Here was a man naked and in chains and living in tombs who wondered if Jesus had come to torture him! I don't know about you, but I cannot think of much more that could have happened to him. What torture is there left to do to a guy in that condition?

People bound in the darkness of today's world also approach Jesus with fear. Why? What torture is left? Many, like the Gerasene demoniac, are already living a tormented mental and emotional hell on earth. How much more can go wrong? How much worse can things get for their marriages and families? Evil has already gotten in. The people who come into revival services with that pained look on their faces have lost their sense of spiritual direction, and so get it backwards: "Is Jesus here to torture me?"

The Body of Christ is tortured and tormented more than we know, not by Jesus but by evil spirits—from pastors to laypersons to deacons to elders to nursery workers to bus drivers to greeters to worship leaders to altar workers. We are incapable of fighting the powers of darkness on our own. We desperately need the power of God.

What Do You Fear?

When I first began to pastor, I saw the side of ministry most people do not see, which pastors do not often talk about in public. More than once Kathy and I were swept away in the backwaters of conflict within the Church—disloyalty, dishonesty, distrust, pride, destroyed relationships. Our roots became intertwined with other people's roots, and when the enemy came in and those people tore themselves away, everyone was hurt.

More than once demonic forces stole in as gossip. Talk was easy and razor-sharp. People carelessly said what they wanted, and rumors circulated about my leadership. Some people said I would not allow people to wear shoes in church! Others said I refused fellowship with anyone who did not tithe. Someone started a rumor that I went to people's houses and filled out their tithe checks. Others said I had left my wife, that this was my second marriage, that Kathy had left me—all of which was untrue. I began to realize this was as much a part of "normal" church life as ministry and fellowship. When I mentioned it to other pastors, they usually shrugged, as if it were part of the bargain.

Since revival came, the accusations have become more fanciful and bizarre, and are even approved quietly by a few pastors.

This is part of what leads me to believe that some of the Church, like the people in the gospel account, is adapted to the work of demons. We are so far from the true God that when He comes to scatter the darkness from our hearts, we grasp fearfully onto the chains of bondage that have held us.

The Gerasene townspeople had Jesus in their midst. They could have asked Him anything—to pray for them, to drive away all the demons in their vicinity, to stay awhile and teach them. But because they were afraid of the wrong things, they walked up to the Messiah and asked Him to leave.

It seems to me that we should rejoice when people get free of the control of darkness—but many in the modern Church scowl. Like those in Jesus' day, we have grown accustomed to the powers that bind us. We are used to the feel of spiritual chains around our ankles and wrists. We wake up and go to sleep with darkness coiled around our hearts. We are accustomed to our bondage and want others to be bound, too.

Imagine what Peter's face must have looked like as the scene unfolded. He was excited because the demonized man was free and able to hold cogent conversation. As the townspeople streamed over the hill to see what was going on with those pigs, he probably expected a great reception, with hundreds of new disciples. At least they would hold a feast or invite the disciples to dinner. Peter probably stepped in front of the eleven, chest out, eyes sparkling. Then he got the shock of a lifetime. The townspeople were upset at the sight of the demonized man, now restored, sitting at Jesus' feet, and they said, "Jesus, we want You to leave town—now."

People who have experienced personal or corporate revival know Peter's disappointment. Because when God gets hold of your faculties, the right things begin to strike fear in your heart again.

Loose talk scares me now as never before. Gossip scares me. Backbiting and betrayal scare me. Worldliness scares me. Lukewarmness scares me. Pride in the pulpit scares me. The love of money scares me. Selfishness in the face of the Holy Spirit scares me. These are common features in the Church today that ought to scare all Christians. In fact, panic ought to set in: "Hypocrisy is wrong! Hypocrites don't go to heaven. We've got to change!"

Instead Bible-carrying people are afraid of revival. And we like to blame the world for everything until it makes us feel righteous. We are willing to point the finger at anybody—drunk drivers, homosexuals, abortionists, politicians, filmmakers—as long as our own faults stay under the cloak of night.

The Gerasene people should have repented and said to themselves, "Here was a man with a legion of demons in him, and we were used to him. In fact, we didn't like it when he changed. Something must be wrong with us. We've got this thing backwards." But they were controlled by fear. Fear makes you reject the Savior to His face.

Fear is never more prevalent than in times of revival, because that is when the enemy, who is in danger of losing ground, works most strenuously against us. He re-awakens the standard human fears:

- Fear of losing control
- Fear of losing friends
- Fear of alienating family members
- Fear of seeing what's really in our hearts
- Fear of being free

If we are to be afraid, let's be afraid of the right things. Everything that could possibly go wrong in the Church already has: suicide, drugs, adultery, fornication, lying, stealing, lukewarmness. There is literally nothing left to fear. Nor have we anything to lose when the old system crumbles—yet because of fear we cling to it.

Instead let's fear the right things, and not sit in judgment on someone who truly gets free, proclaiming that it cannot be God. Let's be people who prefer light over darkness.

Jesus' Response to Rejection

What is the end result when we are so afraid of light and so adapted to demons that we will not let Jesus work among us? Look at the end of the story:

> [Jesus] got into the boat and left.
>
> Luke 8:37

He did not argue or give them a sermon or try to persuade them that the demonized man was better off. He did not say, "Let Me do one more miracle, and I'm sure you'll change your mind." He simply left.

Many people may have gone their whole lives to churches that have pushed away the power of God because it scared them. Long ago Jesus walked out the front doors of some of those churches without performing a single miracle, and the people continued as if they did not even know He had left. The pastors kept whitewashing the tombs instead of opening them up and exposing the darkness inside.

You can judge your own adaptation to demons by the response of your heart when Jesus comes to help you in times of personal or corporate revival. Ask yourself:

Are you afraid of Jesus?
Do you accept that fear as the guiding force in your life?

Do you judge Him according to your own emotions rather than by the fruit His work produces?

Are people you know being set free? If so, how does that make you feel? Threatened? Insecure?

What exactly is causing those feelings inside you that resist God's love?

Listen to God's Word:

> The light shines in the darkness, but the darkness has not understood it. . . . He was in the world, and though the world was made through him, the world did not recognize him. He came to that which was his own, but his own did not receive him.
>
> John 1:5,10–11

What does it say about us when our knee-jerk reaction is to push Jesus away? Can it be that we are more adapted to demons than to God?

We need to ask God to transform our minds, open our spirits and make us hungry and thirsty, so we adapt ourselves to God, not demons. Take authority over any demonic powers in the strong name of Jesus. We cannot let years of acculturation to a dark world blind us when the Kingdom is breaking in. That mistake was made countless times throughout the Bible with God's prophets, apostles and His very own Son. They were simply not recognized for who they were. People were driven by demonic forces to kill God's greatest representatives, often in the name of established religion.

If we reject what God is doing in the current outpouring, ignoring the fruit and embracing the fear, we will fall into the same tragic pattern.

As you adapt yourself to God, you will radiate more of His presence—perhaps to such a degree that even strangers will notice the difference! Instead of the general darkness that engulfs mankind, people will see light in your eyes. Instead of insecurity, you will exude confidence. Instead of a halfhearted approach to life, you will be full of zest. People may come up to you and initiate conversations—at the bank, at the supermarket, at your kids' school functions—not because they like your clothes or your hairstyle, but because they want to be around Jesus.

You will become an aperture through which they see the Kingdom of light, and that Kingdom will break in on them—through you.

7

Thirsty?

On the last and greatest day of the Feast, Jesus stood and said in a loud voice, "If anyone is thirsty, let him come to me and drink. Whoever believes in me, as the Scripture has said, streams of living water will flow from within him."

John 7:37–38

MANY of us are familiar with the words being used to describe the current move of God. They have a river theme. We talk about flowing in the move of God and of being in the river. Rivers bring wonderful images to our minds—swimming and laughing, splashing, feeling carefree and playful.

In recent decades, by contrast, some pastors have tended to treat churches like corporations, which is a terrible simile because corporations are impersonal and absolutely no fun. Even worse, every corporation has a CEO, who usually corresponds to the pastor, and God is edged out to the margins. In the "corporate church" model, people are in control and the environment is businesslike, sanitary, professional, competitive and stressful.

Who wants church to feel like a job or commercial enterprise? I am all for professionalism, but I do not think God wants pastors to feel as though they are going to work on Sunday mornings. And He wants church to be natural, revitalizing, relaxing—a place where people are free to be who they are in Christ without criticism or competition.

The great thing about a river is that only God can direct it. He brings forth water at the source and, as it runs along, He brings streams in from all sides to add to its size and force. I have been to other revivals, and know Smithton is experiencing a stream different from those. I like the analogy of different streams flowing into the river of God because different places will not react the same way when the power of God comes. We can flow with others, however, and let the Lord incorporate all the streams into one river. Indeed, we have to, or we will frustrate the work of God.

The idea of revival is popular right now, even though it means different things to different people. Many Christians are sincere in their desire to know God and are willing to let go of earthly treasures and security. Some are merely curious. Some consider revival a fad. You see ads in magazines or on television for seminars and conferences and schools of this and that. Everybody is having a revival explosion and inviting you to attend. There are books, articles, videos. Smithton, too, has had its share of media attention. But when the religious establishment, the Christian media and all the publishing companies get hold of something popular, including a move of God, they tend to want to harness its energy and growth because they feel they have found something that sells. Revival is selling, and whenever something is selling, people take advantage of it to make money.

Granted, I would rather that revival be as popular as it is than for people to reject it entirely. The problem is, God's work is ever changing and moving forward. If we try to keep it in the same groove, we will stop the progress of God's will on earth. We may sell books and magazines and videos for a few more years, but the life will have slowly ebbed away, and what once was a great move of God will wash ashore like a beached whale.

I say this because I believe that the revival of today is moving beyond the boundaries we have laid out for it. The river is jumping its banks. It is not in the character of God to take us halfway or to act in predictable ways. He wants to lead us from glory to glory, and each stage is different and better than the one before.

Not all churches, however, will allow this. Some will get stuck in this revival, trying to relive the way it currently looks and feels, even as they claim they are moving forward. I have seen it happen already with churches trying to accommodate the current revival rather than flow with it. A lot of what flies under the banner of revival is really the same old preaching turned up a few notches on the sound board, and the same old services, just longer and more often.

It is not the form of revival that will change people. Nor will Friday night services change people if they keep doing the same thing they have been doing on Sunday mornings. Where is the fruit? If the confusion, lack of power, lack of commitment and slackness remain, then the message is obviously not speaking to the people of God where they are.

Just as people raise their voices when talking to foreigners in hopes it will help them understand, some preachers yell out words ineffectively. These are words God is no longer using. He wants to say something new to people, but He needs to find willing mouthpieces.

Thirst Is First

Every new move of God in our lives has a starting point, but most people these days, whether in revival or not, do not know where the starting point is. They think the outpouring begins as a river or stream. It does not. It is especially confusing when God comes powerfully to one church but not another. The people of church number two may try to copy the outward forms of church number one, and may get to the point of simply waiting around for God to show up—a kind of sanctified fatalism.

I am convinced that a river does not just pour out of heaven spontaneously. Many today are talking about the great river that is coming, but they err if they want to start with the river or stream, and that is not the order Jesus gave. According to Him, the outpouring starts with thirst.

We have looked in the last three chapters at three problems characteristic of the Church today: our desire to remain in control; our preference to build our own houses rather than God's house; and our remaining in the iron grip of fear. But the biggest problem regarding the outpouring of revival is not lack of water, but lack of thirst. Once you get that revelation, you realize God will move wherever people are thirsty. You will not find a single place on the planet where He will stay His hand if there are thirsty people. But He is not wasteful; He will not pour out on people who do not really care. There is no reason to blame the Father for not giving us water when we are not really thirsty.

I am not talking religious-thirsty or pretend-to-be thirsty or half-thirsty or curious-thirsty. You cannot be thirsty for a mixed drink and expect God to deliver. God is not a bartender for our varied whims. He goes for pure things—unleavened bread, pure water. But many professing Christians are drinking from all sorts of different streams, not just God's stream. They drink from the television stream, the past-hurts stream, the philosophies-of-the-world stream, the self stream, the greed stream—and then they try to drink from the Lord's stream. They squint their eyes and sing loudly and raise their hands and wonder why revival is not breaking out in their churches.

Why not? Because these professing believers have quenched their thirst in other ways.

God will not stop you from filling your bottle at different streams, but your drinking choices will stop Him from moving in your life.

Most people want Jesus at least a little bit; revival comes to people who want only Jesus. God looks for a conviction of the heart that says, "I don't need the world. I don't need anything but You, Jesus. Any time not spent on You has been wasted. I'm willing to do whatever I need to do to get You back into my life."

Back in the early 1980s Kathy and I were touring with my family in a music group called Jubilation. We had gotten past the difficult years of staying in people's homes and driving away from churches emptyhanded. Churches were finally putting us up in hotels. We had repeat engagements. My music was charting on the radio. But during our last year of touring, I began to feel empty. More and more churches seemed to have less and less of the Holy Spirit's work.

In 1983 we went to an Assembly of God church in Omaha, Nebraska, where Winkie Pratney had just been teaching a series on revival. Someone there gave me cassette tapes of the series, and as we drove to Michigan I listened to them over and over, hearing for the first time about Jonathan Edwards, the Welsh revival, Evan Roberts and Charles Finney. Tears streamed down my cheeks in the dark Greyhound bus. The words stirred me, broke my heart, convicted me and drew out a yearning. I realized I did not have what those men had—and thirst began to develop inside of me.

I had lived with that thirst for many years, but watched as disappointments sapped my energy. We had started praying for a great outpouring in October 1993. Every Tuesday night, for more than two hours, we would cry out from our hearts for God to bring revival. Now, two and a half years later, I see it was the grace of God that brought me to a low point just before revival came in 1996. I was willing to do anything, leave anything, go anywhere and give up anything to get God back in my life. I was sick of drinking from other streams; my thirst for Him was purer than it had ever been. To this day I do not care if I ever preach again, but I have to have Jesus.

When I finally surrendered myself to Him totally, a river of life sprang forth in my being such as I had never known.

The River Is Real

The river of God offends some because first it flows into people and then it flows out and spills all over the place. Some people do not want to watch other people flowing like a river. The King James Version says it so well: "Out of his belly shall flow rivers of living water" (John 7:38).

We live in a day when rivers are flowing out of people. Folks may react differently. Some fall and shake; some never do. Some yell or moan; some are silent. The ones with little physical response may think everyone else should have little physical response, too. The ones who react violently may wonder why other people are not affected the same way. There is plenty of potential for criticism. But when you get a bunch of people together who are really thirsty, they do not care what is happening to anyone else; they are busy drinking.

It is the critics—the ones not drinking—who stand back and point fingers. They have nothing else to do. When you are drinking, you leave the judging to God and get lost in His presence. The last thing you want to do is make fun of people. It is wasted time.

It is impossible to ignore when the living water of Jesus flows from your belly. This is not a passive experience or one that can be tucked away or overlooked in the middle of a service. When living water flows out of your belly, you feel it. I expect that when that power flows through people, they may do some flaky or inappropriate things. But what is even flakier and more inappropriate is faking or mischaracterizing the river.

When I am in church and the Holy Spirit is about to move, I feel wonderful jolts of life in my belly. Sometimes they are so strong that I actually bend a little when they hit. They are like stirrings of love and joy. Many, I know, can attest to the same feeling. Smith Wigglesworth said it well when he looked at Niagara Falls and commented, "That's what is going on inside of me."

Some people come to Smithton just to watch people respond to the living water flowing out of them. Some leave here saying, "This is too much for us," but turn their cars around a mile down the road and come back. Their brains cannot handle it but their spirits are thirsty.

The invisible stream is real because Jesus said it was. He was not playing make-believe, nor setting us up for something that does not really exist. Many of us have heard the words of Jesus quoted over the years—"Out of his belly shall flow rivers of living water"—but fewer have lived it. When it happens to you, you say, "Whoa, that's new!" Until it happens to you, you do not realize it is even missing.

Feeling things in your belly is not limited to the presence of the river flowing there. All of us have felt this sensation in different forms. When a police car pulls up behind you, lights flashing, you feel it in your belly. When you were in grade school and forgot to do your homework, you felt it in your tummy. When some bully was threatening to beat you up and all day you were anticipating it, you were sick to your stomach. Most of us have felt fear, anxiety and dread in our guts before. Yet when good things begin to pour out of the belly—which, unlike fear, anxiety and dread, are biblical—it is somehow controversial.

I do not know about you, but I have been on the negative end enough. Now I am ready to feel the roar of life rather than the roar of fear. That is why I like what Jesus said in Revelation 2:4: "You have forsaken your first love." Anyone who has been in love knows the feeling you get in your stomach. It begins in the belly and grabs your whole being.

There was a time before I met Christ that I drank alcohol every day of my life to deal with my feelings. In the first two hours of drinking I was covering up feelings; after that I was creating new feelings. And when I had nothing to drink, especially on weekends, I panicked because my feelings were out of my control. On Saturday I would buy enough alcohol for Sunday, because back then, where I lived, you could not buy liquor on Sunday. On Christmas Day I would drink all day and go to church to have Communion with my family. I could not even celebrate Christmas without covering up certain feelings and evoking others.

The point is, many of us use external aids to create feelings, because on the inside we are dead. Pornography represents the extreme of this. Romans 1 talks about losing all sensitivity and turning to sensuality.

If you want God's river to flow in you in greater measure, you must thirst for more before He brings it. How do you develop thirst for God? One way is simply to think about who He is and what He has done—not just in your own life but in the lives of people throughout history. Reading the Bible stirs up your spirit to know God; hearing or reading testimonies of others passionate about the Lord can also awaken new thirst.

If you seem to have no thirst at all, which is not uncommon, pray that God will give you that thirst, and He will. You may have to pray for a while—a subject we will discuss in a later chapter devoted to praying for personal and corporate revival—but God will certainly answer and give you a thirst that will enable you to pray with more fervor than ever before.

I am thankful that God has given me the ability to feel again—life and death, sadness and joy. We have great music in our services, but I am stirred up long before I get there. I can sit in a room alone now and cry tears of joy just thinking about people or the Lord or what He has done in me. And it does not take seeing Old Yeller die for me to feel sadness.

Some people have never tasted from the river of God. Some have sampled and drunk, then stopped being thirsty. Others are trying to get the river to flow without checking their thirst level. If there is no river, there is no drinking; and if there is no drinking, there is probably no thirst. Jesus says to get the order right. It all begins with thirst. Then the river flows in us and out of us to other thirsty people all over the world.

.

Part 3

Receiving the Kingdom

Keys to Revival

"Arise, shine, for your light has come, and the glory of the LORD rises upon you. See, darkness covers the earth and thick darkness is over the peoples, but the LORD rises upon you and his glory appears over you. Nations will come to your light, and kings to the brightness of your dawn."

Isaiah 60:1–3

If a worldwide revival hit us, would we recognize it? Are we in tune with God enough to see it coming and declare when it arrives?

I remember years ago driving and listening over and over to those tapes about revival. Though I longed for it, I did not know exactly what it would look like. The Church was enamored then of big meetings in non-church settings—festivals, conferences, seminars and retreats. Thousands of people would flock to convention centers for a "Holy Spirit Explosion." I believed that revival would come in local churches. Even so, I could not predict what it would be like.

At Smithton we talked frequently about revival. We planted seeds of revival in each other's hearts. We began to ask ourselves, What does revival look like? How does it sound? How does it make us feel? What does it

103

do to our hearts? How are homes affected? How are children affected?

The revival we were pondering is here, and I am the first to admit it did not take any form I would have expected. It is far more wonderful than I imagined—more comprehensive and loving, more powerful and real.

Isaiah begins the above passage of Scripture with two key words, *arise* and *shine*. He was prophesying that the scattered Israelites would be brought back to Zion—but I think this was also a prophetic picture of worldwide revival. If so, then the first activity revival causes us to do is "arise."

Arise and See the Glory!

It is much like the woman Jesus spoke to who "was bent over and could not straighten up at all" (Luke 13:11). He said, "Woman, you are set free from your infirmity" (verse 12), and she stood up straight for the first time in eighteen years.

The sinfulness of this world acts like gravity on the inner man, pulling us down to the point that most of us, spiritually speaking, are bent over. We may raise our hands and even jump and clap and show outward signs of being alive in Christ—but on the inside we are stooped.

One of the first things to happen when the Kingdom of God breaks in is that we rise out of that stooped position. Suddenly we have hope and can view the world as we were meant to. We see the possibilities inherent in the Kingdom; we see Jesus more clearly; we see other people in light of who God made them to be.

To arise is to be restored to the perspective God created us to have. It lifts us from the mire of discouragement, powerlessness and hypocrisy and gives us a glimpse of an entirely different future. The inbreaking Kingdom has a gravity all its own. It is an upward pull on the spiritual man that counters the effect of sin and radically alters our outlook on life.

This happens notably in three areas—first, in the Church. When God's power begins to pull us out of our stooped positions, we see that the Church is meant to be entirely different from what we have made it. Rather than a weekly conglomeration of people with individual agendas seeking to have their personal needs met, it is a body of believers functioning in mutual interdependence, trust and love.

We begin to see our need for the Church, our place in the Church and the centrality of the Church to life in general. No longer is the Sunday morning service a stage show where entertainment is of the highest value, or a feel-good seminar, or a massive self-help session, or a small corporation with a CEO pastor and his employees. No, when we arise, Jesus comes to shepherd His little flock, and all our adoration is directed toward Him. No one else is exalted, no matter how effective his or her ministry. Church services focus once again on interacting with Jesus, giving Him worship and honor, allowing Him to speak to us, heal us, convict us, love us.

A church that has arisen is real. Nothing phony can exist there anymore—not useless rituals or societal habits.

The second outlook that changes when the Kingdom of God breaks in is our view toward our homes. When we arise at the touch of Jesus, we see new possibilities in our home lives. Just as transformation takes place in our churches, so our families begin to take on the character of Christ rather the character of the culture. We realize the family was not created for entertainment or for the fulfilling of individual agendas; it is the basic unit in the

Body of Christ. God has a plan for each family just as He does for each church.

The third change in outlook involves our personal lives. Not long ago a man rode a bicycle to Smithton from St. Louis—a two-hour drive by car. He had to sit in the overflow section; then, as it turns out, he slept in the yard. He went through all that trouble because he wanted so desperately to be in revival. He had been spiritually bent over for so long that he was willing to do almost anything.

That man is one example of thousands of Christians who, after years of being dragged toward the ground, have heard God say from heaven, "You may have made all kinds of mistakes, but now it is time for restoration. Arise!"

Although the glory of God's presence is something He alone controls, there are a number of things we can do, as individuals or churches, to arise, to open ourselves up to the glory God wants to bring into our lives.

Let Jesus Sweep the House Clean

As we arise with the outpouring of true revival, we find an increase in the presence of the glory of God. There are many religions in the world, but it is the glory of God's presence that distinguishes the people of God from everyone else. Moses learned that the glory of God's presence is the believer's mark of distinction. He asked God, "What else will distinguish me and your people from all the other people on the face of the earth?" (Exodus 33:16). We must believe that God wants us to live in His glory, and we must resolve not to continue trying to move forward without it.

We looked in chapter 2 at the living, prophetic picture of the cleansing of the Temple. When Jesus upset the furniture—and the financial network that had grown up around the religious rituals—He was foretelling the destruction of the Temple some forty years later. Tradition has taught us that the issue was selling merchandise in God's house. For this reason some churches today are careful to make sure tapes and books are sold in the foyer and not in the holy sanctuary.

But to think we can escape the righteous indignation of Jesus by selling our wares in a different location of the church is absurd. The issue that enraged our Lord was not selling merchandise but cheating others. His motive, I believe, was deploring the lack of the distinguishing mark of God's glory in that place.

He does not object to our making life more convenient. It was certainly a lot easier for those traveling to the Temple from long distances to buy their sacrifices and supplies when they arrived, rather than have to bring everything with them. But Jesus was concerned that the place of honest communication, the house of prayer, had been turned into a place of dishonest gain—a den of robbers. There was no distinction, in other words, between the people of God and the rest of the world. The dishonesty of the streets had invaded the Temple.

Jesus' attitude has not changed. He still comes to overturn the tables when what is inside is no different from what is outside. Although we sing "Amazing Grace" on Sunday mornings, if the same greed and lust and selfish ambition can be found inside our churches that we find in the world, then our tables need to be overturned.

We see this further clarified in the story of Simon the Sorcerer in Acts 8, who offered money to buy the Holy Spirit's power. We may wonder how anyone could be so stupid. But we make the lesson too shallow when we think it has to do with money. Verse 21 reveals the real problem: "You have no part or share in this ministry, because your heart is not right before God." The offer of money was only a symptom of a heart gone wrong, and Simon was told to "repent of this wickedness" (verse 22). What wickedness? The wickedness of offering money? Partially, but the root of the problem was that Simon thought he could have a share in the ministry without a right heart before God.

This verdict extends way past the first century and into our day. While evangelists preach shortcuts to heaven and pastors coddle congregations at offering time, the wickedness of Simon the Sorcerer flashes like a neon sign. How could any of us be so presumptuous as to think we could have any share in the work of the Holy Spirit when our hearts are not right before God? While we claim our citizenship in heaven, our behavior shows little difference from that of the average family man or career woman. The desires of the flesh, the lust of the eyes and the pride of life are all too often the real rulers of our hearts.

Jesus Christ came as the first of a new race, declaring that those who would follow Him would become like Him. This new race was to be different from all the other people on the face of the earth.

If we are to have a worldwide renewal or awakening, if we are going to arise, then we in the Church must become a distinct people marked by the glory of God's presence. A walk into the house of God should be like leaving the world of night and entering the land of day. It is bad enough to have to deal with the darkness in the world; no one should have to face it in the Church.

If we want revival, therefore, we must allow the Holy Spirit to sweep our houses clean and allow Him to set His priorities.

Seek the Kingdom

In Matthew 6:33 Jesus tells us to seek first His Kingdom. This is an absolute necessity for any person or group wanting to arise and see God's glory. *To seek* means to run after and pursue, and *first* means first. Nothing in all our lives must be allowed to take a higher priority.

The lesson from Jesus is that we must not allow desire for material provisions to get in the way of the Kingdom, nor worry to interfere with our first commitment. In fact, Jesus gets right to the point and shows us the difference between a pagan and a believer: Pagans run after food and drink and attire and believers do not (see verse 32)! Jesus suggests that seeking God's Kingdom and His righteousness first is actually the cure for anxiety and worry. He even appeals to our logic: Why run after things like pagans when by seeking the Kingdom first, the provisions will come to us (see verse 33)?

If we want God's glory to come, every congregation with a desire for revival must set a priority to seeking the Kingdom and Jesus' righteousness first. If we do so with all our hearts, the glory of God's presence will indeed rise upon us.

Eliminate the Competition

There is another story in the Bible that helps us arise. It is when the rich young ruler asked Jesus in Matthew 19 how to get eternal life. When the Teacher suggested that the place to start was by keeping the commandments, the young man insisted he had kept these all his life.

"What do I still lack?" he asked (verse 20).

At this point Jesus presented a different agenda than most of us have. He answered, "If you want to be perfect. . . ."

Perfect? Who said anything about being perfect? I just want to know I am saved in the sweet bye-and-bye, that

I have a home in heaven after I die. I just want eternal life. What is this perfection stuff?

"If you want to be perfect, go, sell your possessions and give to the poor, and you will have treasure in heaven. Then come, follow Me" (verse 21).

The statement hit not only the young man but all those listening like a sniper's bullet. The young ruler had no words left to say and no more questions to ask. His only response was to walk away sadly.

To us in a materialistic society, this can be a pretty scary moment. Most of us who say we want to follow Jesus would not be willing to part with our wealth—of whatever magnitude—in order to do it. (Those who do not have much may be tempted to want a lot of this kind of preaching; maybe some of the wealth will land in their laps!)

Preachers down through the ages have tried to figure out a way to make this story more palatable to their congregations, but the interpretation is clear and simple. At heart it is not about money or wealth or possessions, nor is it a story that strikes fear only in the rich and leaves the poor alone. Jesus is letting us know that He will not compete with anything else in our lives.

The message then and now is the same: If you want to walk the perfect walk, if you want all the benefits of the Kingdom, if you want to live in the glory of God's presence, you must eliminate the competition. The lesson is not about disposing of wealth; it is about seeking God's Kingdom first.

If you want to gain eternal life and be perfect before God, begin now to eliminate the competition from your life. Jesus would not compete with wealth for the young man's affections. What is His competition in your life? It can be a person or a possession or a pursuit. Whatever it is, Jesus will not compete with it. And if we do not eliminate it, God's glory will not rise upon us.

Stop Living for Yourself

The glory of God is a strong element at the Smithton Outpouring. At the time of this writing we have been meeting five days a week for three years. I cannot think of a service since this all began in which the glory of God was not present. Oftentimes it becomes so thick and heavy, it feels as though Jesus has come and placed His royal robes on your shoulders. It is a common experience to find yourself bowing forward. It is not only that Jesus is worthy of such reverence, but you can actually feel the weight of His glory. As Isaiah said, "The glory of the LORD rises upon you."

That glory does not come cheaply or by accident. The condition of our hearts is the major determining factor.

A recurring theme of the Smithton Outpouring comes from 2 Corinthians 5:15: "He died for all, that those who live should no longer live for themselves but for him who died for them and was raised again." We live without the presence and glory of God not because He will not participate, but because we want to possess all while still living for ourselves. Let's read the Bible not just to marvel at what God did in the past but to see how godly men and women lived, so we may follow their examples. Contrary to modern ideas, they did not live in a different dispensation; they lived with a different disposition. If we would ever begin to live as they lived—not for ourselves but for our Lord—we would find that what God will and will not do in our day changes dramatically.

At Smithton we have found that as our devotion to Jesus increases, His glorious presence follows. We must arise not only toward the light that is coming, but against the darkness of a self-centered life perpetuated by a self-serving gospel.

If we will allow Jesus to sweep our houses clean, seek the Kingdom first, eliminate the competition and stop living for ourselves, we will arise and find that the glory and presence of God are returning to the people of God.

Shine, for Your Light Has Come!

After God has helped us arise, straightening us from our stooped positions, we begin, in the words of Isaiah, to shine.

How do we shine? What does this mean, exactly? Is it something mystical or strange? Do we have to glow like Moses or have physical manifestations or experience signs and wonders? What do we actually do after we have arisen?

It is not as strange as some people think. Mystical things may happen in revival, but they are not the emphasis. One time a nonbeliever came into our church and stood in the back for a while, observing. Suddenly he ran out, terrified, and, as I heard later, told people in town, "Don't go to that church! There are angels running up and down the aisles there!" I have not seen angels doing that, but he had seen a sign and a wonder.

Still, God's glory does not come by signs and wonders; it comes from the basics. When the Kingdom comes, it does not bring new teaching, it revives old teaching that we have forgotten.

Repentance

Shining comes from loving the basics of what Jesus told us to do. One of the best ways to get revival is to repent. Jesus said, "Repent, for the kingdom of heaven is near" (Matthew 4:17). A revival of repentance renews the light and glory of God.

I have gotten invitations from some denominations to speak at their conventions. They ask me to come because they want revival. I think they expect I am going to bring some great revelation they have never heard before—some mystical thing that happened to us that can be replicated in their churches. But what has really brought revival to Smithton and many other places is the repentance that took place long before the power of God came. There is not much more to it than that.

When people arise out of a stooped position and see the reality of their lives, they are crushed because of their lack of devotion to Jesus, and from the depths of their hearts comes a wellspring of repentance. The Holy Spirit Himself shows them their sins and shortfalls, and they naturally cry out for forgiveness. Repentance is a moment when the spirit cries out, "I've failed You, Lord, in my lack of devotion, in my faithlessness, in the doubleness of my heart, and I can't change by myself. Please help me!"

There is simply no revival without repentance, period.

Prayer

To shine you must also have a revival of prayer. We do not need a revival of dreams and visions, though people are having these more and more and we should welcome it. We need a revival of people who are so broken and so determined to grasp the Kingdom that they pray heart-felt, gut-wrenching prayers.

Recently at a prayer meeting in Smithton, during a move of God's Spirit, I sensed Him saying, *I want to hear urgency.*

O.K., I thought. *Urgency about what?*

The Spirit of the Lord spoke again. *I don't care what you pray about. You can pray about this revival. You can pray about somebody's finances. But tonight I want to hear urgency.*

God was reminding us what urgency sounds like and what true prayer feels like, and He was guarding us from the trap of repetition.

Let's have depth of prayer. Let's be people who want a move of God so badly that we will come together and turn ourselves inside out for it! (In chapter 13 we will talk about revival praying.)

Worship

Another part of shining is to have a revival of worship. When God's people overflow with adoration and thanksgiving without shame or fear, day after day, the light and glory of God begin to come.

You must be a worshiper. You cannot struggle with worship and say, "I don't feel like it." Get over it! Worship God the way the Bible talks about. Every Hebrew reference to *worship* involves a posture of the body. So lift your hands. Lie on your face before the Lord. Kneel before Him. Bow before Him. Pour out your heart to Him. At our meetings we all jump and raise our hands and pump our fists into the air, not because it looks good but because that is what our hearts are doing. We allow our bodies to express what the inner man is feeling when it contacts God.

A large part of worship is honest exuberance before God, unhindered by concern for reputation or embarrassment. When our hearts are really focused on the King of kings, we do not care what the person next to us is doing or how she worships the Lord, and we do not care if anyone sees us or what he thinks. It is wonderful to experience and maintain liberty in worship!

Love and Forgiveness

Shining also requires us to experience a revival of love and forgiveness. These are essential. If you want revival, you cannot wait for the other person to apologize; you must forgive everybody, regardless. You cannot wait for people to be lovable; you have to love them, regardless. Release every hurt, every grudge, every petty hatred, and start lavishing love on everybody, including your enemies. I do not want to make this seem complicated, so I will leave it at that.

Rediscover the highest commandments, according to the Son of God:

> "'Love the Lord your God with all your heart and with all your soul and with all your strength and with all your mind,' and, 'Love your neighbor as yourself.'"
>
> Luke 10:27

Revival consists of the simple things we forget about—repentance, prayer, worship, love and forgiveness. If you do those things, your heart will become soft and tender toward God and His Kingdom.

People these days are arising and shining because their light has come and they are experiencing God's glory personally. The glory is not in the sky somewhere or in a cloud or in a special room among a super-spiritual elite. The glory is all over average people! Like Moses their faces are lighting up.

Moses arose and shone because the glory of the Lord descended on him. Jesus shone on the Mount of Transfiguration because the glory of God had come to Him. I see reflections of that glory all over people in my church when the glory of God comes upon them. Today's revival has caused many to arise and shine, for our Light has come.

9

Holding Your Position

So then, dear friends, since you are looking forward to this, make every effort to be found spotless, blameless and at peace with him.

2 Peter 3:14

"I know your deeds, that you are neither cold nor hot. I wish you were either one or the other! So, because you are lukewarm—neither hot nor cold—I am about to spit you out of my mouth."

Revelation 3:15–16

ONE of the major deceptions hindering revival in the Church is the idea that we need not put forth effort in our walk with Christ. In fact, many of us have been trained by the religious system to be afraid of the word *effort*. "You can't save yourself," certain teachers argue—and have argued for five hundred years since the Reformation.

Yet the Bible says (as we see in the passage from 2 Peter above) to "make every effort to be found spotless." Does that mean we save ourselves? No. Does it mean our good works will reserve us a place in heaven? Of course not. It means God is holding out salvation to us, but we have to make the effort to grab hold of it. No one was ever born again by accident. And once we make the effort to reach out for salvation, we must make every effort to live a spotless life.

Through twenty years of serving the Lord, I have found all the promises of God to be that way. We have to lay hold of everything He wants us to have.

Today revival is being held out to us, but we have to make the effort—and keep making the effort—to live in it. The failure to understand this has caused frustration and despair in many parts of the Body of Christ.

Soon after I was saved, I served in a denominational church. I was so on fire for God that some people actually told my colleagues, "Don't worry about him. He'll cool off. They all do." I do not know if it was my backbone or my stubbornness in God or something else, but I decided that was not going to happen.

Twenty years later the observers are still waiting and, by God's grace, I have not quit yet. But I do not blame them, because they spoke out of their experiences. People often get on fire for Jesus only to drift away. This happens in great part because we do not understand the notion of effort in regard to our spiritual walk. Or, to look at it another way, religion has actually put us in a bind with regard to effort!

Martin Luther took us from one extreme to another. In fact, he did not help us as much as some Protestants think he did. There were some believers alive at the time who could have helped a lot, like the Anabaptists. They wanted to go all the way, from reformation to revolution. Luther wanted to go only so far. To his credit he stopped many people from crawling on their hands and knees on glass, thinking they were pleasing God. But he also created a new mindset that said, "If you want to walk with God, don't do anything."

Ever since, some Protestants get the jitters the moment anyone starts putting any effort into his or her walk with God. "Quit striving," they say. "You're trying to earn your salvation." But we have removed the necessary work of maintaining a right relationship with God.

Much of the work of revival, then, goes to reversing the damaging legacy of the Protestant Reformation. Today God is saying, "Haven't you had enough of dull, dead, effortless religion? I am sending you a revival and it is yours forever—if you make the effort to keep it."

Relationships Require Effort

Most of us have learned by now that our salvation comes solely from faith in Jesus Christ. But every mature person also knows that the way to maintain a relationship is to put effort into it. Without effort relationships falter. They lose their steam. Any relationship in which we do not expend energy cannot last.

We all know what it is like to be in love. We fall head over heels for that special someone, who falls head over heels for us. But many married people find after a while that the power of those giddy feelings fades. We long wistfully for the days when we were dating, and we assume that now we are past the height of our relationship—forgetting that relationships take work to grow.

We do the same with our religion. If we have been saved for a while, we imagine that we have reached the heights with God, and this is as good as it gets. We confuse giddy feelings for the depth of maturity. We have romanticized our salvation experience to the point of denying the greater, deeper power that God has for us as our relationship with Him grows.

Salvation, like marriage, is the beginning of a journey in which it is vital to maintain the relationship. There are lots of ups and downs and mistakes, but with effort come attraction and power and unity and excitement. When effort ceases, people naturally begin to stray or fall away, or become resigned to a dead relationship. Sometimes they actually get divorced from their first love.

I have noticed something over the years: Divorce never happens to people who try too hard. Marriage-splitting arguments seldom result from the words "You loved me too much" or "You were too generous to me." Divorce comes from neglect or a lack of effort or just allowing self-centeredness to rule.

When we remember this, Peter's admonition for us to "make every effort to be found spotless, blameless and at peace with [God]" makes more sense. Right away most of us are knocked in the face with a new idea: *I have to put forth effort to make my relationship with God go somewhere!*

The same idea has hit me a number of times. I grew up in Nazarene and Methodist churches. I was first called to preach in a small Nazarene church in Hays, Kansas, when I was five years old. It was no emotional thing. The service was over; I was all by myself in the sanctuary. And with nobody else in the room, God called me to preach. I ran to the altar, crying my eyes out. The pastor and my dad came in and said, "What's wrong?" And I said over and over, "I've been called to preach."

It was not until age 23 that I broke through to my destiny. My wife and I knelt down in my mother's family room, ten miles from the church I now pastor. Mom and my sister, who had been powerfully healed in the charismatic renewal, prayed with us. I gave my life to Jesus, and Kathy and I were filled with the Holy Spirit.

The first words I said after I stood up, without any forethought or premeditation, were, "God has called me to preach"—the exact words I had uttered as a five-year-old. I realized then that God had called me much earlier, but I had put forth no effort.

No one ever fell away from God because of trying too hard or loving Him too much. No one ever became lukewarm because of giving God too much time or praying too long or dying too much to self. That is why Peter exhorted his readers to "make every effort to be found spotless, blameless and at peace with [God]." Most of us are in the spiritual condition we are in because we have been in a dead relationship with God. We did not maintain it. We became *lukewarm*—harking back to the other Scripture at the beginning of this chapter, and the trait we are enjoined to avoid.

Sure, we gave our lives to Jesus. We made a lifelong commitment. We promised what we would do for Him. But at some point we neglected those promises and went back to our selfishness. Putting minimal effort into the relationship, we allowed the lukewarmness around us to cool us off.

Look at Our Role Models!

Peter went on in his letter to warn us to be on guard against "ignorant and unstable people" (1 Peter 3:16). I do not know a pastor who does not want to print this on a banner in his church, because ignorant and unstable people are everywhere, and not just in churches. They are in factories, in stores and on the job. They may call themselves Christians or they may not, but they are responsible for drawing people away from their first love.

Ignorant and unstable people are the ones who say, "Be careful, you might go too far. There's no power today. That might be of the devil. Be careful, be careful, be careful." These people put a huge damper on people's efforts to stay close to God. Suddenly we are being careful of the wrong things—the very things God wants for us as believers.

Certainly we are supposed to be on our guard, but against ignorant and unstable people, not against the power of God! How many people do you meet who say, "Sounds like God is really doing something powerful in your life! Make every effort to go all the way with Him. He's worth it. Leave everything else behind." More likely we hear the mantra, "Be careful," and our effort withers like a scorched plant.

Second Peter 2:17–20 continues the godly warning:

> These men are springs without water and mists driven by a storm. Blackest darkness is reserved for them. For they mouth empty, boastful words and, by appealing to the lustful desires of sinful human nature, they entice people who are just escaping from those who live in error. They promise them freedom, while they themselves are slaves of depravity—for a man is a slave to whatever has mastered him. If they have escaped the corruption of the world by knowing our Lord and Savior Jesus Christ and are again entangled in it and overcome, they are worse off at the end than they were at the beginning.

I have watched lots of people give their lives to Jesus. Some went on with Him and some did not. I have watched many be filled with the Spirit. Some went on and some did not. But I can tell you this. Almost every time people receive Jesus and feel His love and know they are born again, they are ready to give up everything and witness to everyone about the resurrected Lord. How long that goes on may vary. But gradually these earnest folks fall into compromise—the same compromise that made the Laodicean church in the book of Revelation lukewarm. (More about that in a minute.)

We get saved and set on fire for God and come into church and sit down and look to the left and right, and up to the pulpit, and suddenly we are surrounded by what 2 Peter 2:17 calls "springs without water." These waterless springs are the Christians! They have been in this longer than we have, so we figure they know better. Everywhere we look, everybody claims to have what God wants us to have—but the springs are dry. It is as if our fellow Christians are walking around with cups full of dirt saying, "Here, drink this." They boast religious words and phrases and say, "Follow me, I've got the way." They claim to believe in God's power. In fact, they believe in a tradition that began in God's power. But it grew cold.

The result is, we fall for a cozy, costless, lifeless religion. We give in to so-called followers of Christ who would rather be at a ballgame or movie or at home watching TV than with Jesus. They are not against church; there are just a lot of other things they would rather be doing. These people become our models.

How Secure Are We, Really?

When we remove effort from the picture, what is left? A country club mentality, an organized charity, maybe— but not a church. Peter further warns, "Be on your guard so that you may not be carried away by the error of lawless men *and fall from your secure position*" (2 Peter 3:17, emphasis added).

This is not a subject we hear many sermons about. But Paul said, "But I am afraid that just as Eve was deceived by the serpent's cunning, your minds may somehow be led astray from your sincere and pure devotion to Christ" (2 Corinthians 11:3).

Thus we see that it is possible to lose both our "sincere and pure devotion" and our "secure position" in Christ.

We do well to remember that Satan, as Lucifer, also had a secure position in heaven at one time. I suspect he realized that God was not going to exalt him the way he wanted, so he became lawless and led a rebellion. That is what lawless people do. The error of lawless men is to recognize no laws or rules and to do whatever is right in their own eyes.

Charismatics and Pentecostals are guilty of their own subtle form of lawlessness, but they call it the Spirit of God: "The Spirit led me" and "God told me to do" this or that. Many prefer not to be part of a church body because it demands that they act corporately and submit to the headship of Christ. As they try to exalt their own talents and egos and giftings above Christ, they commit the sin Lucifer committed.

Lucifer's example shows us that he was not able to maintain his secure position, and neither were one-third of the angels who were thrown out of heaven with him. Satan knows all about Jesus, but there is one thing he will not do: He will not make Jesus Lord. Satan knows the truth as well as any of us. His problem is, he does not have the heart to make Jesus Lord over himself, and he denies Christ's power over him.

This is where the real battle lies. We may claim a secure position in Christ because of our knowledge of Jesus. But that puts us in no better company than Satan and the fallen angels! The only reality separating us from the power of darkness in this world is the Lordship of Jesus Christ.

Anyone who has been in church for a while, especially Pentecostal or charismatic churches, has heard a sermon from Revelation 3:16 in which Jesus is about to spew, spit or vomit the lukewarm believer out of His mouth (depending on how badly the pastor wants to shock the congregation). People in the pews say, "Amen!" as though this is some action movie, and the villains are lukewarm Christians, and God is the hero who gives them their due. But I am convinced we do not treat this "spewing" as a reality. It has become almost a myth or legend in the Church—something that happened way back when, or something that will happen far into the future. We consider our own positions secure and treat God's judgments as either past or future tense.

But God does things in the present, too, and all Christians must fight for their first love—or lose it. When Jesus says He is about to spit people out of His mouth, and then the people do not change, I believe He does it. I have known a lot of lukewarm people in my life, and I figure God has done it over and over, and many do not even know it has happened. They listen to the sermon in which Jesus threatens to spit people out of His mouth, and relish the thought of the lukewarm people being punished, when in fact they themselves have already been vomited out. They do not take lukewarmness seriously enough. They act as though God will hold the lukewarm in His mouth for two thousand years, savoring the taste.

God does not do that. He warns us what He is going to do. Then He does it.

At-Risk People

The result of lukewarmness and of not making every effort to keep ourselves spotless is that these traits create at-risk people. Judas Iscariot was an at-risk person. There he was, working in the power of God to heal the sick and cast out demons. But he had the disciples' purse in his hand and was stealing money from the Twelve. Though he was doing religious things and trying to follow Jesus, his hand was still in the world. He was only partially committed.

As a pastor I know how many at-risk people are in churches today. They have one foot in the Kingdom but a hand still in the purse or a mind full of deceit. Some are still justifying their sins or blaming their parents or their Sunday school teachers for their problems. When the pressure is on and their inner selves are revealed, the truth comes out—and it is wicked.

The good news is, God makes room for repentance so that we do not fall away: "Bear in mind that our Lord's patience means salvation" (2 Peter 3:15).

Peter is not just talking about people needing to repent of their personal sins. Our present concept of repentance is Americanized and heavily skewed toward individuals rather than toward the body of believers. To many, repentance means reciting our faults to the best of our ability, hoping we did not miss one. Some may actually have an idea that at the end of time, God will say, "You did pretty well, but there were a few sins you just plain forgot about. Remember these?" And you will say, "Oops," and He will say, "Sorry, you're going to have to burn in hell forever."

That is silly, of course, but it is the reduction of the way many of us think about repentance.

No, I believe Peter is talking about corporate repentance and about running away from a doomed, lukewarm and at-risk system. If you read this passage in context, you see that God is trying to get us to repent from a system that will be melted by fire. A person can say, "I'm sorry," a million times and walk right back to the worldly system that has judgment marked on it, and his fate would be the same, because he has become like all the other lukewarm people in the system.

We must repent of a lifestyle that has fed us, ignored God, centered on values and ideas contrary to Him, and supported the world mindset that nailed Jesus to a cross. This is what we are turning from. We cannot love the system that killed Jesus and then be saved by Him! It makes no sense.

How can you fall from a secure position in Christ? If you do not maintain your relationship with Him and if you follow the error of ignorant and unstable people who distort the Scriptures by saying that a walk with God requires no effort.

During these days of revival people ask me all the time, "How do I hang onto this so I don't lose it again?" The answer is, *By effort.* Effort in prayer. Effort in worship. Effort in time commitment. Effort in giving. It may sound basic, but God will not lead us to greater things until we master the fundamentals.

Why is effort so important? Because we put effort into what is important to us. No effort means no importance. A zealous effort is appreciated by our Father because it says that what is important to Him is important to us, too. God wants His Kingdom to be ours, for our ways to be His. Making effort in prayer, in singing, in attendance, in giving and in relationship keeps us from the lukewarm and draws God's attention.

What made Jesus different? He never stopped putting forth effort. Even now He lives to make intercession for us at the right hand of the Father. So take a hint from Jesus: Increase your effort, your time, your energy level—and the presence of God will increase with it.

10

No Backsliders in Heaven

"The nobles send their servants for water; they go to the cisterns but find no water. They return with their jars unfilled; dismayed and despairing, they cover their heads. The ground is cracked because there is no rain in the land; the farmers are dismayed and cover their heads. Even the doe in the field deserts her newborn fawn because there is no grass. Wild donkeys stand on the barren heights and pant like jackals; their eyesight fails for lack of pasture." Although our sins testify against us, O LORD, do something for the sake of your name. For our backsliding is great; we have sinned against you.

Jeremiah 14:3–7

SUPPOSE we asked this question in a Bible quiz: "Is there any place in Scripture where God says not to pray for a certain people?" Most people would answer, "No, God would never say that." But when God spoke to Jeremiah a few verses after the passage quoted above, speaking of backsliders, He said:

"Do not pray for the well-being of this people. Although they fast, I will not listen to their cry; though they offer burnt offerings and grain offerings, I will not accept them. Instead, I will destroy them with the sword, famine and plague."

verses 11–12

Evangelicals have created a category that does not appear in the Bible: the backslidden Christian. The Bible talks about backsliding, but we have given this concept our own twist in order to soft-pedal sin and make it appear that the Church is growing.

We love to hold evangelistic events in which hundreds come to Christ, because it makes us feel as though we ourselves are O.K. and that the current religious system is bringing others into the Kingdom. So for decades we have counted how many come to the altar to give their lives to Jesus Christ—not distinguishing those who actually leave the altar with the true life of Christ in them. In so doing we are counting the people going to the cistern but not those who leave the cistern with water. Thus, when certain respondents begin "backsliding"—falling away from Jesus—we keep their numbers in church growth records as proof of the growing Kingdom.

It matters less whether a person attends church on Sunday morning than whether he or she also attends on Sunday night or Wednesday night and is following Jesus in between times. Really committed people are not just popping into a service once a week; they are living daily for the Lord.

How do we know who is leaving the well with water? Who is receiving the Kingdom week after week? We look at the fruit of their lives. Do they persist in their sins? Are they controlled by worldly influences? Have they found freedom in Christ? Many who go to church every week in search of water come out "with their jars unfilled" (verse 3).

In spiritual terms the United States is in a drought. The thing about a spiritual drought is that it does not affect just the people who "deserve" it; it affects the entire land. That is why the opening passage from Jeremiah mentions plants and animals. They are innocent, but even they are affected by drought.

Those Who Leave with Their Jars Empty

What is the cause of spiritual drought? Whether it be the one in America or the one in Jeremiah's day, the cause is the same: "Our backsliding is great" (Jeremiah 14:7). Drought comes when the leaders and people are backslidden and when the outward picture—toting Bibles, going to church and singing worship songs—does not match the inward reality. So we invent new categories to fit changing definitions of commitment.

All you have to do to be categorized as a radical, on-fire Christian is go to church three times a week and participate actively during the song service. But if you show up only now and then, and if your belief in Jesus has little effect on your life, people categorize you as saved but backslidden.

The problem is, these definitions are not biblical. Nowhere in the Bible do we find backsliders who are at the same time Christians. We find passages that talk about running the race, fixing our eyes on Jesus, putting our thoughts and minds on things above and doing everything we can for the Kingdom, until the trumpet sounds when "the dead in Christ will rise first. After that, we who are still alive and are left will be caught up together with them in the clouds to meet the Lord in the air" (1 Thessalonians 4:16–17). You cannot be sliding backward and going upward at the same time!

We can only conclude that there are no backsliders in heaven. There never have been and never will be. "Backsliders" who are only names on a church roll do not go to heaven. Backsliders will not receive one ounce of the Kingdom in this life or the next.

But that sounds to some people like blasphemy. They look at Jeremiah 14:9, in which the backsliders say, "You are among us, O LORD," and think that gives them a way out. But one verse further we read that these backsliders "greatly love to wander; they do not restrain their feet. So the LORD does not accept them."

The people in Jeremiah's day who turned their backs on the Lord said, "The Lord is among us." But God said, "Though they offer burnt offerings and grain offerings, I will not accept them. Instead, I will destroy them with the sword, famine and plague" (Jeremiah 14:12).

This is a description of God that most people do not recognize. Many have never met this God. They believe they know the one who accepts everyone no matter what he does. This is why backsliders feel so secure in the Church today. They have been coddled by doctrines and theology that never tell them they are backslidden. They have been told that if they believe in the historical Jesus, they will escape all the wrath that is to come.

But the Bible says not just to acknowledge the historical facts of a Man who lived and died and rose again, but to repent and believe. *Repent* does not mean just be sorry. The Bible talks about worldly sorrow that leads to death, and godly sorrow that leads to repentance and salvation (see 2 Corinthians 7:10). Backsliders have been lied to by false prophets more concerned with their status in the worldly kingdom than in God's Kingdom.

Jeremiah saw the same thing happen in his day:

> But I said, "Ah Sovereign LORD, the prophets keep telling them, 'You will not see the sword or suffer famine. Indeed, I will give you lasting peace in this place.'" Then the LORD said to me, "The prophets are prophesying lies in my name.

I have not sent them or appointed them or spoken to them. They are prophesying to you false visions, divinations, idolatries and the delusions of their own minds. Therefore, this is what the LORD says about the prophets who are prophesying in my name: I did not send them, yet they are saying, 'No sword or famine will touch this land.' Those same prophets will perish by sword and famine."

Jeremiah 14:13–15

The people had so many prophets telling them no harm was coming that they were lulled to sleep. Yes, they were concerned with the drought. They did not like the lack of water but they were not concerned with the lies—and the lies were bringing the drought.

Those Who Wander from God

We have seen the plight of backsliders who came to the well to drink but left with their thirst unquenched. We can also use the term *backslider* in another capacity.

When revival began in Smithton, I thought it would be evangelistic in nature, with prostitutes, drug addicts and anyone who had never been saved coming to Christ. But that did not happen. Instead we started reaching people who had once been born again but who had drifted from their faith. Rather than describe this group as backsliders, I began to view them as "the new lost," because they once had known Jesus but had fallen away.

Many Christians use the term *lost* to mean those who have never known Jesus. But in the context of Scripture, the lost are those who once belonged to the Kingdom and who drifted away. You cannot lose something you never had. The world is not lost; the world is dead. When Jesus said He had been sent to the lost house of Israel, He meant that the people of Israel had gotten lost. The Kingdom had

131

slipped from their grasp. The Lord was going out to find as many as He could. Again, in the parable of the lost coin, the coin was lost in the house, not outside the house.

So the lost are those who have been inside the house but who no longer have a relationship with God.

The Prodigal Son, you will notice, was already a son when he became lost. He was not considered lost simply because his father had no idea where he was; he was lost because he was in a dead relationship with his father. When the young man requested his inheritance, it was the same as saying, "Dad, I wish you were dead already." The son wanted out of the relationship and out of the house. When he came to his senses, he planned on asking to be a hired servant—one of those who did not live in his father's house. But, showered with his father's love, he found true repentance and made his father's house his dwelling place once again. With the father-son relationship restored, the son was declared found and alive.

We need to come to our senses and realize there are no in-house backsliders. The new lost are not ignorant of the Father in heaven. They once belonged to Him but wandered off of their own accord—and Jesus comes to find them. He wants to cure them, and us, of our backsliding: "Return, faithless people; I will cure you of backsliding" (Jeremiah 3:22).

And we must not lie to backsliders anymore. We have to stop telling them they will receive the Kingdom, just in smaller measure. We must acknowledge that God has brought drought for a reason—to get us to see our backsliding so that He can provide the cure.

11

Our Lives for Your Lives

> "Our lives for your lives!" the men assured her. "If you don't tell what we are doing, we will treat you kindly and faithfully when the Lord gives us the land."
>
> Joshua 2:14

FEW Old Testament stories grab my attention like the story of Rahab and the spies. It has great significance, I believe, for how we view the Kingdom—and our identity as Christians.

First we see that Joshua learned something from his previous involvement in spying: Don't send twelve men to do it; otherwise they may come back divided! He sent only two. And when they got to Jericho, they decided to spend the night at the house of Rahab, a prostitute.

Such a course of action would be scandalous today, but I wonder if this was not a wise decision for the two spies. There was probably so much traffic in and out of the house that they could be observant without being too conspicuous, and their alibi was good if anyone was suspicious.

The plan, however, did not work. The king of Jericho learned that Israelites had come to spy out the land, and some of the king's scouts went right to Rahab for the scoop. Then we have one of the great moments in biblical history, as she told the king's men, "The spies went thataway!"— and for the moment the two Israelites were saved.

Why did she do it? Because she knew the Lord had given the land to Israel.

What tipped off this otherwise unremarkable woman— this outcast, this immoral element in society—that the Lord was giving the land to the Israelites? We probably cannot answer with any certainty. It is even more baffling when we consider that forty years earlier the people of God had proved faithless although they had seen miracle after miracle. They had seen the Red Sea parted and all Pharaoh's horsemen and chariots drowned, yet they still did not understand what God was up to.

In any event, Rahab knew. She told the spies:

> "I know that the LORD has given this land to you and that
> a great fear of you has fallen on us, so that all who live in
> this country are melting in fear because of you."
>
> Joshua 2:9

And she asks them to swear that they will show kindness to her family, because she has shown kindness to them.

The spies, willing to repay her with life for life, make an agreement with Rahab to spare her and her family. You remember the story. She is to hang a scarlet rope out the window so when the conquering Israelites see it, they will spare her house and its inhabitants from the destruction that will fall on Jericho.

The symbolism of the scarlet rope unmistakably fore-shadows Jesus Christ. The rope was a sign of salvation to both the Israelites and to Rahab, to the chosen people of God and to anyone else who would believe.

Crucified with Christ

In the midst of this imagery of Christ, we come to the words that sum up the entire Gospel and give us a clearer view of the Kingdom:

> "Our lives for your lives!"
>
> Joshua 2:14

If we really understood this principle, very few of us would go through life with messed-up theologies or half-baked ideas about following Jesus. This is the entire point of what Jesus preached. He preached a message of repen-tance, not just so that we could go to heaven and live hap-pily ever after, fishing in the stream of eternity. He ex-horted us to repent because "the kingdom of heaven is near" (Matthew 4:17). We are to pick up our crosses, therefore, and follow Him.

Paul put it this way:

> "I have been crucified with Christ and I no longer live, but Christ lives in me."
>
> Galatians 2:20

And:

> I urge you, brothers, in view of God's mercy, to offer your bodies as living sacrifices, holy and pleasing to God—this is your spiritual act of worship.
>
> Romans 12:1

These notions collide with our Americanized minds because we miss the deal Jesus offers: "My life for your life."

In more instances than we care to admit, we advocate a "ride-into-the-sunset" idea of salvation: "Just say the prayer and believe what Jesus says about Himself, and you'll be saved. That's all it takes."

This is partially true—we are saved by grace, through faith. But when we twist certain parts of the truth, we make lies out of it—what theologians call heresies. The great American heresy, as we have discussed in previous chapters, is salvation as a one-time mental decision and not as a lifestyle lived from the heart. We must remember that we are called in Christ to die.

The other day I received an e-mail from someone wanting to know my thoughts on when the world would end. I suppose it is easy to develop a fascination with end-time events, but in my experience, the people most concerned about the end of the world are those who fear being judged, or those living in the world who do not want to lose it.

My response to that e-mail was this: If you have decided to give your life to Jesus, then your world has ended already. This fact may have yet to be manifested in the physical realm, but spiritually it is true, because the way of Christ is the way of death to this world.

This is what Paul meant in Galatians 2:20 when he said he was crucified with Christ. And he made the same point when he explained:

> Forgetting what is behind and straining toward what is ahead, I press on toward the goal to win the prize for which God has called me heavenward in Christ Jesus.
>
> Philippians 3:13–14

Paul did not mean forgetting past hurts or wounds, as an American victim mentality would have us believe. He was talking about his entire life, the good and the bad. What made the men and women believers of the New Testament great was that they had already experienced the end of the world. Today we often try to live in two worlds, living as close to the edge as we can, preserving what we can from our worldly lives while still getting Kingdom credit.

This is not the way it works. Jesus says, in essence, "I have given My life; My blood was shed for you. I was crucified and was the first to go. Later you get to enter in. But first I get your life." This is where we can miss the Gospel of Jesus Christ and the blessing of the coming Kingdom. This is why we do not experience revival power and the fire of God and the miracles we read about in the book of Acts.

If we try to skirt the issue and say, "I want Jesus to die in my place, but I also want to keep my life and order it however I please," the agreement breaks down and the power of the Gospel is nullified. Here is when churches become filled with lukewarm believers and with backsliders and with arguments and splits—because it becomes just another manmade institution. The Kingdom does not break in on such places because, like the Gerasenes, many of us send it away.

When the Kingdom came for Rahab, the least likely role model in the Bible, she seized it and hung on for dear life. Christians today might stand back to judge revival and weigh it, perhaps thinking of the risks. Not Rahab. She reached for God's Kingdom with all she had, dying in the sense that she turned her back on her own people and forever abandoned life as she had known it. She said, "This is my only chance. I know the Lord is coming to deal with His enemies. I'm throwing my whole life in with you Israelites."

In that moment this unknown outcast became a hero of the faith. The deal she struck with the spies went down in history as an example of emptying oneself for the sake of salvation. Everyone else in town may have been melting in fear because of the Israelites, but Rahab reached for the Kingdom, and it saved her life.

A Binding Agreement

Now comes an interesting corollary to dying with Christ. As Rahab helped the two Israelite spies escape out the window, they said to her,

> "This oath you made us swear will not be binding on us unless, when we enter the land, you have tied this scarlet cord in the window through which you let us down, and unless you have brought your father and your mother, your brothers and all your family into your house. If anyone goes outside your house into the street, his blood will be on his own head; we will not be responsible. As for anyone who is in the house with you, his blood will be on our head if a hand is laid on him."
>
> Joshua 2:17–19

Not only is the story of Rahab a great example of giving one's life; it is also a prime example of saving it. The purpose of this agreement for both parties was to ensure that they live. This death-life contrast might sound like a contradiction until we realize that the Gospel offers us not only the mandate to die but the opportunity to live. Jesus died a substitutionary death; now He asks for a substitutionary life—yours and mine! In other words He substituted His body for mine and died; now He wants me to substitute my life for Him and live. The divine exchange—a life for a life.

Jesus is saying, "I want your life because I have to live through someone to make this work. I will be with the

Father; you will stay down here. And for centuries people will be born and reborn, and I will live through them, until My death is shown to be the greatest victory of all time—not because I died as I died, but because the Father raised Me from the dead, and I can live as I live, through other people." Part of the miracle is that somehow Jesus can live through people who have not died.

> To them God has chosen to make known among the Gentiles the glorious riches of this mystery, which is Christ in you, the hope of glory.
>
> Colossians 1:27

It is not enough to agree mentally that Christ died for us. Even the devil (as we noted earlier) believes that. The difference is, we believe this simple, straightforward fact to such a degree that, like Rahab, we throw ourselves fully into the Kingdom. We give up our lives freely and let Christ live through us, because He died and rose again to fashion us, to work through men and women, generation after generation, to show the ultimate wisdom of God. When we miss that point, our religion becomes silly and selfish.

Ephesians 2:1–2 says:

> As for you, you were dead in your transgressions and sins, in which you used to live when you followed the ways of this world and of the ruler of the kingdom of the air, the spirit who is now at work in those who are disobedient.

Verses 8–10 get into the familiar territory:

> For it is by grace you have been saved, through faith—and this not from yourselves, it is the gift of God—not by works, so that no one can boast. For we are God's work-

manship, created in Christ Jesus to do good works, which God prepared in advance for us to do.

The plan from the beginning of time was that, while Jesus is physically absent from the planet, the Holy Spirit uses us to do the works Jesus would do if He were here. Somebody will say of me now, "He's preaching works!" Yes, absolutely. I believe strongly in works—after being saved by grace, through faith. We have been prepared in advance not to be an audience for a preacher but to do good works.

God's Craftsmanship

Two and a half hours from where I live is the city of Branson, Missouri, and a theme park called Silver Dollar City. Here old crafts and trades of the Ozarks have been brought back to life. As you walk through the streets of this simulated nineteenth-century American city, you see woodworkers shaving logs down into toys and tools, glassblowers making animals and hummingbirds, blacksmiths banging out metal items on an anvil. All around you are people crafting items by hand, taking great care while pursuing their vision relentlessly for the completed project.

Those craftsmen remind me of our heavenly Father. He fashions each of us by hand for a beautiful purpose. He is not willing to go the modern way, using cheap plastic or gluing us together haphazardly. Sometimes we want God to throw a ministry together, or a marriage, or a family, or a church, or a revival. But He is a craftsman who makes works of art. God shapes us masterfully to do the works we were created to do.

Our commitment to Jesus is a commitment to be crafted, to be fully surrendered. That element can at times be lost.

You remember James and John asking Jesus, "Let one of us sit at your right and the other at your left in your glory" (Mark 10:37). Jesus responded, "You don't know what you are asking. Can you drink the cup I drink?" (verse 38). In other words, "You want the place that I have, but are you willing to live the kind of life I live?"

Everybody is asking God for revival. Sometimes I wonder if Jesus is repeating for our ears, "You don't know what you're asking!" Revival is not party time—an opportunity to dance and shout and have a good time. The coming Kingdom is a disruption and exchange of lives. It means laying down our lives and letting Jesus live through us as He pleases.

Rahab's agreement would not have worked had she betrayed the spies; her life would have been forfeited. Likewise we cannot betray the commitment we have made to Jesus Christ and assume that His part of the agreement will still be in effect. The only way the agreement is binding is if we are found in the house of commitment on the day of salvation. If we are out in the world, we will not be saved. We must be in the Body.

The Gospel was foreshadowed in one beautiful moment by a prostitute and two spies: "Our lives for your lives!" If you can get this, you get the Gospel. When you get the Gospel, you get the Kingdom. When you get the Kingdom, you get the promises. And when you get the promises, you get everything. Everything you need for life and godliness will be yours.

Part 4

Working for the Kingdom

12

Practical Steps to Encourage Revival

SOME people have a wrong idea about revival. They think God sends it primarily to passive receivers. In fact, according to this view, hungering for revival or working toward it actually makes revival illegitimate, while it is super-spiritual to think that God simply moves sovereignly and does everything for us as He wills.

I call this the "sky-is-falling" approach to revival—people standing around waiting for it to happen. There is no scriptural basis for this notion. Just the opposite! It ignores the example given us in parables in which the workers or sons were required to labor and produce fruit. And it overlooks Paul's advice to Timothy "to fan into flame the gift of God" given him by the laying on of Paul's hands (2 Timothy 1:6). Nor did Paul ever say to wait around for the day of the Lord!

Revival, like the Christian life, is participatory. It is not we as audience and God as performer. In the Old

Testament God lit the fire on the altar, but He instructed the priests to keep it going. In revival God lights the flame, but we are instructed to fan it with prayer, worship and repentance, to name a few. We have already discussed some ways we deny our own responsibility to put forth effort for revival and the Gospel, and we looked in chapter 8 at what we are to do—repent, pray, worship, love and forgive—once God has touched us supernaturally and brought us up from a stooped position.

In this chapter I want to show five steps we can take to help encourage the arrival of revival. The story of Nehemiah offers excellent teaching regarding cooperating with the Kingdom.

1. True Assessment

Nehemiah was the kind of guy who was not willing to wait around for things to get better; he wanted to be part of the solution. I like Nehemiah because he was a seeker of God, passionate but also practical. In the beginning of his story we see him looking for answers:

> I questioned them about the Jewish remnant that survived the exile, and also about Jerusalem. They said to me, "Those who survived the exile and are back in the province are in great trouble and disgrace. The wall of Jerusalem is broken down, and its gates have been burned with fire."
>
> Nehemiah 1:2–3

The first of the practical steps we can take toward revival is getting a *true assessment*. In chapter 8 we talked about the concepts of "arising" and "shining." Getting a true assessment is how we actually begin to do this. Nehemiah made inquiries of others and surveyed the scene to find out the true state of the people of God. If you do not see that there is trouble, you will not see the need for change.

The reason many of us do not experience God moving powerfully in our lives is that we prefer not to assess our present spiritual condition. We may arise for a moment, but on a deeper level we refuse to acknowledge our need for repentance.

The reason some churches do not see a move of God is the same: They will not take a true assessment of present conditions and do not see their need for repentance. They are so busy hyping their church programs, or trying to impress others with their worship team, or worrying about Sunday school attendance, that they never step back and look at the entire picture. They never acknowledge that few lives are changing or that few people are growing past adolescence in Christ. These churches put ads in the yellow pages describing their congregation as "the church that loves everybody," and visitors leave saying, "I must have gone to the wrong place!"

Pastors are the worst at taking a true assessment because they think it reflects on them personally. I know; I have been there. I discovered that it may indeed reflect on us, but it also reflects the state of the Church as a whole—how we have believed lies and been robbed of the power of God. We cannot pretend everything is O.K. just so long as our denomination looks good, or the church advertising scheme matches up, or the congregation looks happy. We need to confess the trouble we are in. Honesty is the first step.

In Revelation 3:17–19, Jesus enjoins such honesty of the lukewarm church at Laodicea:

> "You say, 'I am rich; I have acquired wealth and do not need a thing.' But you do not realize that you are wretched, pitiful, poor, blind and naked. I counsel you to buy from me gold refined in the fire, so you can become rich; and

white clothes to wear, so you can cover your shameful nakedness; and salve to put on your eyes, so you can see. Those whom I love I rebuke and discipline. So be earnest, and repent."

Notice the difference between what they said and what He said!

Jesus calls us to honesty, to see reality as He sees it, so we can begin to realize who we are, what our church is, what we have been doing wrong. When the presence of God breaks in, we arise and see things as they really are—as Isaiah did when he said, "I am ruined! For I am a man of unclean lips" (Isaiah 6:5), or as Peter did when he said, "Go away from me, Lord; I am a sinful man!" (Luke 5:8).

I have watched preachers proclaim how wretched and lost people are, and the listeners sit there coolly until the service is over and then file out as if nothing has happened. They have been told how wonderful they are for so long that they cannot hear anything else. In churches today people do not realize what they are really like in the eyes of God. But as revival increases, people's self-image changes drastically and they are more willing to make a true assessment.

2. True Concern

When I heard these things, I sat down and wept. For some days I mourned and fasted and prayed before the God of heaven.

Nehemiah 1:4

After a true assessment must come *true concern*. This is the step that takes us from arising to shining, and the lack of it is perhaps the biggest problem I see today. Most people know that churches are not producing the kind of people they should. Our message is supposedly good news, but it must not seem that way to outsiders! It probably appears to them that people have as good a chance at making it outside the church as in. The only difference is, people in church waste their Sunday mornings and blow their money on the church instead of spending it on themselves!

Do we really care about the shape our churches are in? Have we felt the tug in our hearts toward a better way? Nehemiah experienced true concern: He wept for days over the state of God's remnant. He invested himself and his emotions in the problem. He overcame one of the major obstacles to revival: apathy.

When apathy becomes entrenched, it is extraordinarily difficult to remove. It settles sins as habits of the heart and breeds cynical statements like "Nothing ever changes" and "Why should we try something new? The old way works just fine." Apathetic people are the most anti-Kingdom people you will ever meet. They no longer care. On the inside they are dead. *The Kingdom will never come to apathetic people!*

Other people demonstrate false concern, which also leads nowhere. I have seen churches in which certain people run down to the altar and cry and repent in nearly every service. It seems wonderful until you realize that they never get any better. Nothing changes, no matter how much they run down to the altar, cry and repent.

Having watched some of these lives unfold over the years, I can only conclude that they are not really repenting. It is a charade, a religious reaction—maybe one programmed into them. They do not even have to feel genuinely convicted for this response to kick in. They have the right outward response—running to the altar and burying their heads—but they lack true concern.

3. True Conclusion

> "We have acted very wickedly toward you. We have not obeyed the commands, decrees and laws you gave your servant Moses."
>
> Nehemiah 1:7

The third step toward revival is a *true conclusion.* The conclusion we must draw in our generation, as in Nehemiah's generation, is this: The state of the Church is our own fault.

Nehemiah saw how wickedly the Israelites had acted and remembered that God had said calamity would occur if they did not follow Him. Nehemiah noticed how vulnerable God's redeemed were to attack—their walls and gates of protection were gone and their young people were being plucked away by the enemy—and nobody cared. Remember, this conclusion described not the Babylonians but the people of God, His chosen ones. God loved them dearly, but they had wandered from Him and were suffering the consequences.

We hear the same refrain echoing today: "I've gone to Sunday school all my life but I got hooked on drugs." "I grew up in church but I got pregnant when I was sixteen." "I'm a Christian but I've been divorced three times." People look at the Church and say, "Why would I want to be with you? You're no better off than we are! You want me to give my life to that?"

We love to blame the world for our problems, but the world is not to blame. Our walls are broken down. The third part of the solution, then, is to draw the only conclusion we can—that we are culpable. We must realize that He has allowed the calamity to come, and then repent before God.

4. True Decision

God does not bring us through a true assessment, true concern and a true conclusion for no reason. He wants to help us shine, but we must take the next step and make a *true decision*. This is where many of us are right now: in the day of decision. Those who have overcome apathy are moving toward one decision or another—to go for God or to go back to our comfort zones.

True concern engages our emotions, our very hearts. It means we are giving ourselves to combat the problem.

I have already described our point of decision at Smithton Community Church in 1996. I was crushed and hurting but hid it from my people, not knowing that God was dealing with many of them, too. Eventually we went through the steps of assessment, conclusion and concern, and made a true decision: We wanted God no matter what.

Since then I have watched others come to Smithton, or attend meetings we have held elsewhere, and immerse themselves in the river of God. They feel the joy and life-giving power of God and look about as happy as they can look. But as time wears on they begin to appear miserable. Shocked, they may confess to me, "I'm in revival. How come I don't feel any better about myself?" The answer is that revival is reality; it shows us who we really are. We do not deserve a thing from God, and He needs us to realize this before His grace can be fully manifested in us.

The good news is, revival is not intended either to make us miserable or to give preachers license to declare what lowly worms we are! The point is to engage our hearts so that we are invested once again in God's Kingdom and concerned about where we stand in it. Jesus is echoing to us His words to the Laodicean church: "You have seen reality. Now I am counseling you to take My opportunity. Buy from Me gold refined in the fire so that you can become rich, and have white clothes to wear so you can cover your shameful nakedness, and have salve to put on your eyes so you can see. Then you will shine, for your Light has come."

God's Kingdom brings an opportunity to possess gold that you have never had before. When you touch the gold of God, it makes everything else seem small and cheap. You become dissatisfied with any imitation the world has to offer—imitation joy, imitation love, imitation thrill. And you long to share that gold with every person, from the biggest success to the worst loser. Once you have seen reality, it is difficult to go back to the fantasy world.

There is nothing wrong with taking time to make the decision. Ask yourself: Do I want to participate in revival or spend the rest of my life running around the mall eating pizza or being a sports fan instead of a Jesus fan? If you would rather do these things than give your life to the move of God, then cry out to God and ask Him to change your heart and priorities until you become a vessel who glorifies His name in this world.

Nehemiah thought about his decision for four months, then went before the king. Perhaps he waited until he was unwavering in his heart. He was not going to stand before King Artaxerxes with a divided heart. He had made up his mind to give up all of his "me" time. He asked to be sent to rebuild the walls and gates of Jerusalem.

Notice, too, that the Bible does not list any of Nehemiah's special abilities. He was not a prophet, for instance, or a priest. But he made a decision that it was time to change history and asked the king, "Send me to rebuild the wall."

Afterward Nehemiah went to Jerusalem and surveyed the situation, gathered the officials, nobles and priests and put the situation before them:

"You see the trouble we are in: Jerusalem lies in ruins, and its gates have been burned with fire. Come, let us rebuild the wall of Jerusalem, and we will no longer be in disgrace."

Nehemiah 2:17

Nehemiah was looking for his team. He wanted people tired of living in disgrace, who wanted to change what could have seemed a hopeless situation. He had to see if the leaders would be concerned. (There was no guarantee they would be!)

They replied, "Let us start rebuilding." So they began this good work.

verse 18

The leaders caught the vision God had given Nehemiah. Right then the Kingdom of God broke through. None of the walls or gates had yet been rebuilt, but revival had begun because they agreed to rebuild.

If any church makes the decision these men made, it can have revival. It is when you settle for what you have—when you want to fit in so you can have coffee with the pastor—that it is hopeless.

Before revival hit Smithton, I had never conducted a series of meetings longer than Sunday through Wednesday. But by the time we had been meeting for ten weeks, I was considered by some to be a revival veteran! I had no idea what we were doing, but the church leadership had made a decision together to rebuild the walls that had been broken down. People in our church found places of ministry they never knew were meant for them. Our worship leader, Eric Nuzum, could have said, "I'm not sure I want to give my life to revival. I think I'll keep driving the forklift at work and just go home to watch the ballgame." But he chose to rebuild, and now the songs he has written are being heard all over the world.

Revival gets its wheels when people say, "Let's rebuild!"

5. True Battle

The fifth and final step reflected in Nehemiah's practical revival was a *true battle*. After the leaders began to undertake the great idea to rebuild for God, opposition arose.

> When Sanballat heard that we were rebuilding the wall, he became angry and was greatly incensed. He ridiculed the Jews, and in the presence of his associates and the army of Samaria, he said, "What are those feeble Jews doing? Will they restore their wall? Will they offer sacrifices? Will they finish in a day? Can they bring the stones back to life from those heaps of rubble—burned as they are?"
>
> Nehemiah 4:1–2

How I sympathize with Nehemiah! Suddenly we find our hero and his fellow builders being ridiculed: "What are those feeble Jews doing?"

That line has echoed through the centuries in many mutated forms. I hear it on a weekly basis: "What are those people doing, trying to change the world and reform the Church and bring the power of God back? It's ridiculous! They have no experience, no credibility. That's no revival. Who do they think they are?"

If you go for revival, you will hear the same thing. Rejoice when you do!

Many people cannot handle revival because they cannot handle ridicule. Nobody likes ridicule, of course, but it is part of the package. Some people will see you shining and be attracted; others will be repelled and threatened. Jesus said He came to bring a sword; this is what that means.

The problem for Christians beginning to arise and shine is that we have been taught by our insecure society that we must be loved by everyone. People in revival will find they have more friends and more enemies than ever—and the idea of being hated is often foreign to them. Can you live with people resenting you for no reason? That is how Jesus lived. People hated Him without any cause, and they will do the same to anyone on Jesus' team.

Here is what Nehemiah's opponents did:

> They all plotted together to come and fight against Jerusalem and stir up trouble against it.
>
> verse 8

Now the enemies of Nehemiah were acting on their hatred. The problem with God's enemies is, they are often more unified than the Church. I have watched congregations previously opposed to one another come together to oppose the work of God. It is like Pontius Pilate and Herod becoming friends at Jesus' crucifixion.

Opposition will come whenever and wherever revival occurs, and some people will be affected by it. It is surprising how quickly a revival supporter can fall prey to the lies of the enemy and become confused, then divisive. They get hurt. Others get hurt. Everybody has hurt feelings. And suddenly we can no longer enjoy revival because there is an emotional mess to clean up. Where did that come from? The devil. He comes to stir up trouble when God starts moving, and he works through willing people.

In the face of this opposition, Nehemiah thundered his call to revival:

> "Don't be afraid of them. Remember the Lord, who is great and awesome, and fight for your brothers, your sons and your daughters, your wives and your homes."
>
> verse 14

These are some of the greatest revival words in the Bible! Banners should be created with these words emblazoned across them, so people remember what they are fighting for, and that the Lord is fighting for us. We are not fighting so we can have a better worship service or longer services. We are fighting for Jesus and His Kingdom.

Some people oppose true battle because they misunderstand certain passages in the Bible. David announced to Goliath, for example, "The battle is the LORD's" (1 Samuel 17:47). The battle *is* the Lord's, but look at David's example. He knew better than anyone whose the battle was, but he went out and killed not only the giant but opposing armies with his sword.

"The battle is the LORD's" means that victory is sure if we follow through and "fight the good fight of the faith" (1 Timothy 6:12). We know this Scripture, but how many people do *you* know who will fight the fight of faith until they die or are thrown into prison for life? Putting on the full armor of God is not for the purpose of holding a church bake sale or a spaghetti dinner!

Here is how the people under Nehemiah's leadership fought their true battle:

> Those who carried materials did their work with one hand and held a weapon in the other, and each of the builders wore his sword at his side as he worked.
>
> verses 17–18

They had to build with one hand and hold a weapon in the other! Most of us probably would have asked God for a nine-foot angel, but these builders were led by practical Nehemiah, who had made a practical decision and followed it through to the end.

Building with one hand and fighting with the other may be the clearest picture of revival that I have ever heard. In practical terms it means not letting revival take a back seat to anything else in our lives—not friendships, not vacations, not obligations, not business decisions. The Kingdom of God is something to be fought for. Recall Jesus' words in Matthew 11:12: "The kingdom of heaven has been forcefully advancing, and forceful men lay hold of it." There is never a time to let our eyes stray from the prize.

Building and fighting at the same time is also why Paul instructed us to "pray continually" (1 Thessalonians 5:17)—because the work of God does not take a break. While we are doing our part to help the Lord build His Church, we will come under attack night and day, experiencing criticism from friends, family, co-workers, even other Christians. The enemy will come against us with doubt and discouragement, trying to reinforce old habits of laziness or apathy.

God's people must resist the voices of the enemy. Satan particularly loves to sow division among Christians, and his plans have succeeded throughout history and to a great extent today. Division begins most often over nothing. It is not usually a clash of ideas or doctrines but a clash of spirits, and spirits do not care if the argument makes sense or not. We can fight spirits of division by exposing their tricks and reminding each other how vulnerable we are to attack. Unity is of eternal value; winning an argument for its own sake is of no value and is the quickest way to become a tool of the enemy.

Our job in this hour, like Nehemiah's, is to rebuild the walls that have been broken down. We build unity, a shared vision, purpose, calling and destiny. We build with a sense of determination that we will not be stopped. Revival is not a sky-is-falling prospect. God has laid out what He will do when we meet His conditions. Nehemiah made a true assessment, experienced true concern, made a true conclusion and decision, and fought it through to the end.

Sometimes we make the subject of revival so mystical that we remove all the practical aspects from it. No one can manufacture the power of God, but we can certainly hear His voice, as Nehemiah did, and take the path He is laying out before us. It will always lead to a greater manifestation of His Kingdom.

13

Revival Praying

"Ask and it will be given to you; seek and you will find; knock and the door will be opened to you. For everyone who asks receives; he who seeks finds; and to him who knocks, the door will be opened."

Matthew 7:7–8

HAVE you ever had a need but dreaded asking somebody for help? Asking requires a bit of humility. God wants that level of humility in us. In fact, His Kingdom does not operate without it. But asking can also be shallow. If praying people were asked, "What did you ask God for three years ago, and did you get it?" many of us would not remember. And because we tend to forget what we asked God for, there is no training in it.

The culture of the Bible was different from our own. A young man did not go to his father and say (in our parlance), "Give me a five, I'm going out with the guys." And the response was more than, "O.K., here's the money. Now get out of here." Instead of just handing his son a five-dollar bill, the father used the request as an object lesson and asked questions like, "Is this something you just thought of, or something you've really been thinking about? Is this really what you want?" Asking was a time of searching motives. And after it was over, the father would ask, "What did you learn through this?" Asking was training time.

In chapter 8 we talked about a revival of prayer—that we need people in the Church who want a move of God so badly that they will come together and turn themselves inside out for it! In this chapter I want to expand on this topic. The familiar passage I have quoted above is our keynote for a look at revival praying.

We begin by understanding that prayer is a time of revelation, not just receiving, just as the seeking level is different from asking, and knocking is different from seeking.

Seeking with All Your Heart

When you seek something, you run after it. You have to narrow down what you want and pursue it. You do not wake up one day and run after one thing, then get up the next day and run after something else—because pursuing requires a lot of energy. Asking might take only a moment, but seeking is strenuous. It forces us to prioritize and to concentrate. When we go from asking to seeking, the diversity of our prayers drops off rapidly.

I read a lot of history books, and have found that no revival ever came because some guy woke up one day and said, on a whim, "Lord, give us revival." Revival is an event to be sought because God wants to make sure we want it! And choosing to live in revival, as we have seen, is a major decision.

Suppose you got a job offer halfway across the country. You might check out the community and write the Chamber of Commerce. You would probably look into the schools. You would ask questions about the crime rate and housing costs and property taxes and recreational opportunities.

Similarly God wants you to check out revival and know for sure you want it. Do you know what you are getting into? Do you know what it is going to cost you? Do you know who is going to oppose you? Do you know the benefits? Do you know the battles? Many people struggling to experience revival do not understand the depth of seeking. They have the desire but do not engage in the follow-through.

Something is happening, however, that is hard to imagine in the midst of the laid-back religion of America today ("If God wants me, He knows where I live" and "If God wants revival, I guess it will fall out of the sky"). A new attitude is growing. More and more people of faith are coming to realize that it is good to be diligent in prayer and important to seek God earnestly. In fact, that is what God is looking for! Earnest diligence is what distinguishes those who prefer to wait and see what God will do from those who truly want revival—the man or woman after God's own heart who will search for Him, seek Him out and actually chase after Him.

Asking means to investigate, to crave and—I like this!—to demand. It does not mean I make demands of others, but that I place this imposition on myself. I intend to seek Him diligently. I have to find Him. I demand to have to have God in my life. I will not settle for less.

It's Beginning to Happen!

Yearning for God is something new in our churches. More are experiencing a craving to know Jesus, to have a fresh touch of God by the power of the Holy Spirit. You can see it on people's faces. It is wonderful!

I get particularly excited as I see young people yearning for God. Just tonight I watched some teenagers in the service here at Smithton. I could see the demand, the searching for the living God on their faces, in their hands. What an experience!—to watch kids singing with fists in the air. Do you see the difference? We have come a long way from blank stares at hymnals to singing with fists upraised! Such a gesture has no meaning in itself, but it probably represents something going on inside. It demonstrates demand, desire, search. I saw it tonight on those young people's faces.

Nor is it just those kids. There is a movement worldwide in which millions of teenagers are being raised up with a yearning and hunger for God, and they are finding Jesus. Christianity is not dead religion to them or something their parents dragged them to. It is real. Christianity is not sitting on the back row and writing notes to boyfriends or girlfriends. It is a sharp hunger to know the living God.

If you have been watching trends for very many years, you know this one is new. It has almost been as if the realm of teenagers and children was forgotten, up to this point. No longer. The craving for Jesus is touching all ages.

Smithton's Journey

Our church sought God for a long time, as deeply as we knew how—hard prayers every Tuesday night for two and a half years.

We had held a Tuesday evening prayer meeting for years before then, but it had not yielded great spiritual victories. People would come into the sanctuary whenever they chose and kneel and bury their faces in the pews while soft music was playing—which we thought was reverent. Strangely, we never really heard anybody pray. People whispered their prayers. Then, after about fifteen minutes, they slipped out and rejoined the real world. Our prayer meeting was not changing our church, by any stretch of the imagination; it just seemed like the right thing to do.

Then God spoke to our hearts that we needed to revamp our prayer meeting. We were to begin a corporate prayer meeting, which I was to lead.

I did not want to lead it! I was already preaching Sunday morning and evening and Wednesday evening. The last thing I wanted to do was lead another meeting. But I did, and it was the best decision I ever made.

I did not know at the outset how to lead a prayer meeting. Fortunately I could play the piano and sing. So I led choruses; then we prayed for revival to come. We kept our prayers pretty much focused on asking God for more of His presence.

Over the weeks I noticed a pattern. After a few minutes of singing, we would pray out loud for about thirty seconds; then the voices would trail off. So I began encouraging the people the way a track coach encourages a runner. I wanted us to seek God together with our voices.

Then the Lord impressed me that asking them to pray publicly was like asking them to undress in public. So I turned down the lights to make it dark except on the platform, and people began to pray bolder and more honest prayers. I led in worship, and instructed them to continue praying after the songs ended, so that worship blended right in with prayer. When the piano dropped out, I told them, I wanted them to pray with the same strength they sang with, because they were terrific worshipers. Sometimes I timed us, as if we were a cross-country team, and we would pray as loudly and passionately as we knew how for a certain length of time. We began to build up our stamina. Our arms did not grow tired so quickly; our minds did not wander so much.

Every week we did this. "Go. Stop. Pour out your praise. Now let's kneel down and cry out to God. Two minutes, let's go. Now let's pray in tongues and intercede in the Spirit." We began to operate as a unit rather than as disjointed individuals. Our efforts were unified and focused. Clearly not all the prayer was deeply felt; some of it was nothing but work. But we believed God deserved to be honored, that He deserved our best and that what pleased Him was not predicated on how we felt that day. If we came to praise Him, there was no holding back and waiting for our emotions to agree.

Soon I no longer had to act like a drill sergeant. The music would stop and the prayers would go on for a long time. Tuesday meetings became our favorite night because the presence of God began to manifest itself.

At the time of this writing, we have been praying as I have described for five years. To me that qualifies as seeking! What preceded the outpouring of the Holy Spirit at our church was long, hard praying.

I want you to have this hope, too. It is like spiritual exercise. If you seek God continually, soon your body begins to crave it. It actually becomes work to be lazy! If you want a true move of God in your life, in your church, in your town, it must be something you want more than anything else. You cannot fool God. Seeking shows Him where your heart is.

Are you willing to want revival so much that you are willing to pray for the next ten years of your life, seeking and craving without giving up and without getting discouraged?

Knocking on Heaven's Door

We can understand seeking, but what about knocking? Why did Jesus distinguish knocking from seeking, and why did He put seeking and knocking in that sequence?

Actually, I believe knocking is the easy part. It is finding the right door that is hard! There are plenty of doors in the Church: church growth seminar doors, cell group doors, counseling doors, higher education doors, spiritual gifts doors. I know pastors who border on obsession with some of these—but anything that takes our primary focus off Jesus can quickly become a wrong door. You can knock on a method all you want, but it will not give you the right answers. Answers lie not in methods but in a Person.

Churches can spend years developing a program to try to solve their problems, but our church found a door that, when opened, activated the Kingdom of God. We began to see people really converted. We saw deliverance. We saw healing. We became people of purpose and destiny because we chose the door called revival. But we did not knock on every door. We chose purposely.

The fact is, I had made a choice to knock on the door of revival for the rest of my life, and if it did not open, I was through knocking on doors! That is how determined I was. I intended to seek out the power of God in my lifetime, and if we could not have it, I was through with the game. I chose to seek what I had read about in the book of Acts. I asked for it. I sought it. I knocked on it. And when I asked, Jesus answered. When I sought, I found. And when I knocked, the door was opened.

Kathy and I and our team from Smithton went to a church not long ago where the people told us they wanted revival. We poured our hearts into them, but revival never grabbed hold. There was nothing wrong with the people. In fact, while we were there, things seemed to be going great, and I knew they had a chance to experience a true move of God. But it has been more than a year since our visit, and nothing more has happened there.

I had a feeling it was not going to hold, because on my way out after the services ended, I grabbed one of their church bulletins. In it I saw all the directions in which they still wanted to go—cell groups, activities, men's groups, women's groups, drama presentations, bake sales, barbecue dinners. There is nothing wrong with any of these, but they wanted to experience revival with all these other things going on at the same time. What did they get? Everything except revival.

The people in my church, by their own choice, do basically two things in life: They go to work and they come to church. We do not have time to do the things we used to do. We have one goal only: We pray for more and greater revival in the Church. That's it! We narrowed down our praying to learning to ask, seek and knock. And the door to the Kingdom has swung wide open.

When God Knocks

Later in Matthew 7 Jesus put us into a new role:

"Which of you, if his son asks for bread, will give him a stone?"

verse 9

Now the tables are turned. We are not the ones asking; we are the ones being asked. We are placed in the father's role, and our child is asking for something good.

The point is, no loving father would give his child something deliberately deceptive. That is why a true move of God is safe. If we ask and seek and knock, if we examine our hearts and choose Jesus, we never have to fear a counterfeit revival. God will not send something deceptive to a hungry heart. He is not out to trick anyone.

But there is a qualifier. This safeguard is true *only* if we ask, seek and knock. When people want revival without praying, pursuing and running after it, that is a good time to fear a counterfeit revival—because they want a shortcut.

In verse 12 Jesus flipped the perspective around again and ended by saying:

"So in everything, do to others what you would have them do to you, for this sums up the Law and the Prophets."

If you read these verses straight through, you might feel as though Jesus got confused. How did He get from asking, seeking and knocking to the Golden Rule? I think He is telling us that the reverse of asking, seeking and knocking is also true. Jesus wants people to treat Him the way He treats us. He wants to find somebody on the face of the earth who will let Him in when He knocks.

Revival is more than learning to ask and seek. It is when the character of the Father is reflected inside of you, and suddenly you want to do for others and for God more than you do for yourself. That is when true revival comes—when the tables turn and we stop seeking more stuff and more blessings, and we fall on our faces and say, "God, just ask me for something and I'll do it."

There has to come a time when you want to be a vessel through whom God works; when you can lie down and look up at the stars on a summer night and say, "God, ask and I'll give to You. Father, seek and You will find me willing. Knock and I will open my heart to You."

There is nothing like intimacy with the Father! When you find it, you understand what revival is all about and why growing numbers of people want it. It takes steady determination in prayer. Are you willing to give what it takes?

The Power of All

PEOPLE often visit revivals to get an impartation from God. But if they have made no prior commitment or sacrifice to their churches back home, and if those churches have no foundation for revival, the people may experience a sweep of manifestations and enthusiasm with no root in prayer, praise or worship. Whatever happens with them may last five or six weeks; then they will tire out trying to maintain individually what must be experienced corporately.

Years ago our congregation decided to commit ourselves to "the power of all," meaning that we function as a body and not as individuals. We cite as a biblical basis two familiar stories. One is when the Israelites marched around Jericho every day for seven days and the walls fell down. The other is when the early Church gathered in the Upper Room in one accord and the Holy Spirit came upon them. In both of these accounts, nothing happened until all the people were unified.

At Smithton we realized there was no good reason we should not *all* be saved, *all* filled with the Holy Spirit, *all* tithe and *all* experience what God has to give. Instead of having loose ends—including some who did not love God or who could not care less—we went for unity. Seventy-five percent of our congregation praising or praying or tithing was not good enough; we wanted full participation. We knew God's power could not flow fully through a broken vessel. We wanted a revival of our attitudes. That is when God released His power on us— and it was *for* all of us, *in* all of us and *through* all of us.

The Smithton Outpouring, then, is not about a pastor getting a touch from God; it is about a church finally acting like a church.

When I go to another church, I cannot help wondering how close it is to acting like a church. It is hard to miss signs pointing in the other direction.

American churches, for instance, love to put the pastor on a pedestal—which is a dangerous place to be! It breeds hypocrites. Being watched all the time puts a person in bondage. At one church I visited, the pastor (whose house I was staying at that night) was so commanding and looked so spiritual that I was intimidated. I preached my sermon that Sunday and felt it was not much of a sermon. Late that night I realized I did not have a towel. Rather than wake anyone, I located the linen closet, opened the door and found, tucked away behind the towels, a television set. Apparently the pastor was so concerned with his "holy" image that he had hidden it!

Then there is the handful of people who dance or shout or jump or give a tongue and interpretation and make the rest of us feel that something is happening. But they are essentially lone rangers, not part of a functioning church. The reason a church is a church is to function together, not apart.

"The power of all" includes all ages—not just adults and teenagers, but four- and five-year-olds, too. In Smithton there are no coloring books or toys in the sanctuary because everybody is involved. I have visited other places claiming to be in revival where the children seem oblivious to what

God is doing. If there are toys in the sanctuary, it is not a sanctuary and the church is not acting like a church.

Revival is toddlers learning to praise God in the nursery. It is young people being shown how to pray for others and to minister in prophetic praying. It is outcasts coming in. It is children so in tune with the presence of God that they do not need Barney, Barbie and G.I. Joe to occupy them. Nobody is excluded when God is involved.

Decently and in Order

One of the ways revival stays orderly is when everybody works as a unit beforehand. In an "all"-empowered church, nobody can really say that the Holy Spirit told him or her to do something that is different from what everybody else is doing. We have found that the Holy Spirit generally tells every member of the Body to do the same thing at the same time. We all know what is going on because we share the same mind—the mind of Christ revealed by the Spirit.

We praise when it is time to praise, are silent when it is time to be silent and express ourselves freely when it is time to be free. When the Word of God is preached, we all sit and listen. The key to keeping revival an honorable thing is timing and placement. I am not talking about human timing and placement; people have tried that for centuries, and it produces deadness. Timing and placement are issues for the Holy Spirit to decide. Our task is to listen and respond.

Spiritual Gifts

Like other ministers I have had many people over the years try to exercise their spiritual gifts on me. One fellow

169

came up to me one day and said, "I want to pray for you. God says He's got a gifting for you. I'm going to pray that you get the gift of taking offerings." Maybe I should have thought it over more carefully, but I declined the offer! In another service a guy grabbed a guitar case, threw it onto the altar and said, "God says the service is not going to end tonight until we fill this guitar case with money."

People often want to be known for their spiritual gifts. We picture ourselves standing before others giving wonderful prophetic words, as crowds reach out trying to touch the hem of our garments. Some people go around giving "words" to people: "The Lord says you're wonderful" or "You're going to have a worldwide ministry and touch millions with your voice." I meet people all over the country who come up to me after a sermon and say, "I want to introduce myself. I am Prophet So-and-So." A person should not introduce himself as a prophet; he should let others do that for him. If he really is a prophet, we will know.

In Smithton we love the gifts of the Spirit, but we do not want people pursuing individual ministry at the expense of everybody else. Most of the ministry done is practical. When the service begins each night, one hundred people go into action to serve our guests—ushering, parking cars, playing music, seating people, running the nursery, praying and more.

A Corporate Mindset

People in Western cultures worry about losing their individuality. This mindset has infected the Church. When a leader tells a congregation to do whatever the Spirit tells them to do, that leader is asking for trouble. He is saying essentially that the Spirit has many minds and sends different messages to different people. But the Holy Spirit is not schizophrenic or double-minded. When He speaks, it is usually the same message for everybody. If He says, "Praise the Lord," we do not all have to praise the Lord in the same way, but we do all need to praise.

Or worship. We do not all worship alike. Some of us are loud, some quiet, some expressive, some speak in English, some in tongues, some sing, some laugh, some cry, some jump, some kneel. The unity is in expressing ourselves to God simultaneously in diverse ways.

At one church, when the congregation was ready to begin praise and worship, the leader said the typical thing: "Just do whatever God wants you to do." Later, when it was time for the offering, the pastor said, "Give whatever the Spirit tells you to give."

Charismatics love these lines because they make us feel spiritual, as though everyone is hearing from God and making a wise decision. We do well to realize that among us are at least a handful of people who have just gone through the mental battle of whether to go to church or stay home and watch television! These are the people in whose hands we are thrusting the move of God. If we want an awakening that touches the entire world, we should think twice about asking people who are only 51 percent in favor of going to church that night to lead, as if their ears are well tuned to the voice of the Spirit.

Instead of putting the financial and spiritual destiny of a congregation up for a vote at every service, we need simply to do what is right. We do not have to ask God what to do about tithing, praying, praising or giving. The Spirit has spoken on those matters in the Bible. We are supposed to be tithers, prayers, praisers, givers. Tradition tells us that when we put a decision into the hands of everyone, they will do the least they possibly can. The book of Judges repeats the line time and again: "In those days there was no king in Israel; every man did that which was right in his own eyes" (Judges 21:25, KJV). I never trust an outpouring service in which people are encouraged to do whatever they want. No wonder we see chaos and confusion!

I encourage all of us, especially leaders, to get away from the individual mindset of Western culture and return to the corporate mindset of Bible days. A corporate mindset is the reason the Scriptures work so well: They address the Body and show the Body at work. Nowhere does the Bible promote a "do-your-own-thing" mentality.

But Christians love to individualize the promises of God: "My God will meet all your needs according to his glorious riches in Christ Jesus" (Philippians 4:19). But that promise is aimed at an entire church. In verse 15 Paul says, "Moreover, as you Philippians know . . . not one church shared with me in the matter of giving and receiving, except you only." This is group talk—to an entire congregation. When Paul mentions the "account," he refers not to an individual bank account but to the church account.

We are also accustomed to taking Scriptures addressed to groups and individualizing them. The exhortation in Malachi 3:8—"Will a man rob God? Yet you rob me"— is addressed not to individual givers but to a nation. In 70 A.D. the whole city of Jerusalem, and not select individuals, came under judgment. The same thing happened to Sodom and Gomorrah. God talks not only to individuals but to groups—the church at Ephesus, the church at Corinth.

In America we want to pretend that the group does not matter, but if you attend a backslidden church, it will affect what God does in your life. We dislike that because it seems unfair, but that is the context of Scripture.

Still, we are more concerned today with what God is telling *me* than in what God is telling *us*. We try to move into ministry on our own, with no context and no lateral responsibility to people in our churches. And many of us are too independent-minded even to hear God! In so doing we miss the Kingdom. In the Body of Christ we are not to stand out; we are to fit in and do our jobs.

Who is special? Jesus Christ is special. We are working for Him.

Team Ministry

When the Kingdom comes, it makes sense that God would give all of us, and not just a few of us, a new anointing. Pastors accustomed to doing all the praying, all the healing, all the prophesying, all the delivering may feel threatened by this new kind of ministry. But the role of pastor becomes more a function of guiding and training people into ministries of their own.

Without giving the impression that Smithton is the only way a church can function in the power of God, I want to describe what our altar calls look like these days.

After the message, and after we have prayed for everyone to receive Jesus Christ as Savior and Lord, we invite people forward for prayer. They flood the front section as soccer fans vie for coveted space at a game. Some visitors run. Some come with tears in their eyes. It is crowded and noisy. The music is playing, and the power and glory of God begin to increase.

What seems chaotic to a first-timer seems orderly to those who work in the revival night after night. Some on our prayer team pray vocally; others intercede quietly. Those receiving prayer are healed of physical ailments, delivered from bondages and set free in a variety of ways. Some scream and shriek as the chains of Satan are broken, which attracts attention from visitors but not from those who have attended for very long. It is amazing what becomes ordinary after living in revival for even a few months!

Any guest preacher, and I as pastor, rarely prays for people during ministry time, so the focus is not on an individual, which would disrupt the working of God. It is important for people to observe the team effort. When you have unity, you have safety, and God works more powerfully through the body of believers. And because the environment is not fractured, visitors can also become vulnerable before God.

Bringing Freedom

When people from out of town first began coming to our revival meetings, all sorts of fears, ideas and secret sins began to surface in our prayer times. Soon the prayers took on a supernatural power that was far beyond us. We began hearing the same testimony from different people: "When I received prayer, something inside of me left. I can breathe deeply again. The weight is gone." We were stunned to hear this so many times, so we took it as a strategy and began to pray that God would pull up unwanted things by the roots.

People reacted strongly. These were not 45-minute prayer sessions. But in a few seconds or minutes God would yank out a problem by its roots. People told of life-long bondages like lust, anger, depression and abuse being broken instantly.

One young woman came to the front to give a testimony. She kept saying, with tears running down her face, "It's my birthday." This meant nothing to the rest of us until she explained that for the last two years she had tried to commit suicide on her birthday because she hated the thought of living one more year. Now she wanted us to celebrate with her. So we stood to our feet and yelled,

"Happy birthday!" to her. God had loosed her from the grip of suicide.

Incidents like this are not unusual when the Kingdom breaks in. They represent the point of confrontation between light and darkness.

Releasing Prophetic Prayer

Another of the wonderful things God began to do in our prayer teams was release prophetic prayer. Suddenly we knew things about people—not future prophecies like "Someday you will have a worldwide ministry," but prophecies that told people their present condition. Someone might say, for example, "You have been held in bonds of oppression and intimidation since grade school, and they are holding you still. Right now the power of God is releasing you."

This ought not to be unusual in the Christian walk. Jesus told the woman at the well not all that she was going to be, but all that she was, present tense. She, in turn, labeled Jesus "a prophet" (John 4:19) and testified about Him to her neighbors, "Come, see a man who told me everything I ever did" (verse 29). That is why we use the term *prophetic prayer*. It reveals you to you and presents an immediate answer in God's power.

Sometimes the battle that takes place at the altar is not pretty. I was part of a team from the church ministering in another city with at least fifteen hundred people attending. A woman on the team gave a testimony to God's power, and later, during the prayer time, another woman, who was very large, came to her for prayer. She wanted help but she was full of demons and had been abusing other people horribly.

The Smithton prayer team member, who happened to be very small, felt that the task might be beyond her, and came to me for help in praying. But I told her she did not need me for God to work. (I did stay nearby in case something happened.)

As the Smithton team member started praying, the large woman fell to the floor and began foaming at the mouth. The foam changed from white to green. Quickly some people grabbed towels, while others hovered around to block the view so it would not become a show in itself. That thin little prayer warrior continued to do battle with the evil spirits and would not let up. Then, as soon as it had begun, it was over. The woman who had requested prayer, once a foaming mess with fists clenched, lay motionless. Soon she was up and smiling as if nothing had happened, and the prayer service went on.

The next night she came in and was very responsive to the worship, lifting her hands and adoring the Lord. Later that night she was filled with the Holy Spirit and began speaking in other tongues.

I do not think these wonderful things would happen in people's lives if we had not been unified beforehand. For revival to go anywhere, it must capture a whole church; and for God to release prophetic prayer, people must be unified. The coming Kingdom is about the "power of all"—empowering not just a select few believers, but all of us.

15

Where Is the Exit?

ON one trip to Florida, Kathy and I decided to take a day and visit Disney World. We were buzzing down the highway talking about the cost and parking and what we would do first. Suddenly a big sign let us know that the entrance to Disney World was the next exit. It sounded easy enough, but as we approached, something did not look quite right to me.

"This exit?" I said. "Do they mean this exit?"

By the time I had made up my mind, I was in the wrong lane, and there we went, right past the exit.

Now, missing the exit does not mean all hope is lost. It can happen to anybody. What it does mean is a lot of time and wandering around trying to get back.

Suddenly our entire focus had changed. At first we had been excited to find the entrance. Now we were trying to get back to the exit!

The spiritual application is so simple that it can easily be missed. In Exodus 6:6 God tells the Israelites that He is going to bring them out from under the yoke of bondage. Then in verse 8 He says, "And I will bring you to the land." Are you seeing the order? It is great to talk about the Promised Land and how God will give it to us. But first things first. If we miss the exit, we might as well forget about the entrance.

Entrance into the Promised Land, which we see when we study the story of Israel, was relatively easy: God Himself won the battles with the Canaanite kings as the Israelites trusted in Him. The way of entrance simply opened before them—once they exited from Egypt. That was the tough part. And they missed the exit continually because they insisted on bringing the ideas of that pagan nation with them. The Israelites' failure to exit from Egypt is what caused them to lapse into unbelief and die in the wilderness.

Although the story has many lessons, it is clear that God wanted, above all else, for them to turn away from the gods of Egypt and toward His glorious presence. It becomes clear, sadly, that they wanted to leave Egypt not because they were offended by her gods but because they were tired of being slaves and doing hard labor. As you will recall, they crafted a god for themselves near Mount Sinai. When they became the Church in the wilderness, their bodies were in attendance, but their minds, emotions, opinions, deductions, conclusions and, finally, their actions were all Egyptian.

This is what made Moses so great a man of God. He had a luxurious life in Egypt, but "chose to be mistreated along with the people of God" (Hebrews 11:25) rather than share in the pleasures of paganism. Through history there would not be many like Moses who understood the necessity of making a good, clean exit.

The problem strikes home with many of us today. We are not offended by the gods of this world. As a pastor I see the pattern repeated regularly. If you listen to the prayers of most people, you find that what they are really asking for is just a better life in Egypt. Others respond sincerely to an altar call yet are doomed to the same wanderings. Why? Because like many millions before them, they want to try the impossible—to find the entrance without ever making a clean exit.

Modern Christendom has sidestepped its responsibility on this one. We have been so busy talking about the entrance to the Kingdom that we have neglected to explain the exit. Consequently millions of believers are still in bondage—wandering around searching but unable to enter the presence of God. We need revival power and an invasion of the Kingdom of God for us to make a clean break from our past habits, attitudes and ways of thinking. This explains why a clear message on repentance is needed today.

Repentance does not mean to be sorry for what you have done. It is true that "godly sorrow brings repentance" (2 Corinthians 7:10), but repentance itself is a change of heart and direction. Repentance means: "I don't want to live in Egypt anymore or share in the gods of this worldly kingdom. I want to turn from Egypt and from the ways of Pharaoh. I want to enter God's presence. Where's the exit?"

The apostle Peter reminds us of God's order: It is God who has called you out of darkness and brought you into His marvelous light. You must come out before you will ever get in.

What is the word from the Lord to millions of church folks today? It is as though He is saying, "Move to the exit, please. I will take you out. I will bring you in."

Prepare to Exit

I am hesitant even to begin to talk about making a clean break from our past ways of thinking, in order to receive the presence of God, because I am not sure you can find a formula that works for everyone. Yet there are a few principles I have learned by living in this marvelous outpouring that might help some along the way.

In John 3 Jesus had a conversation with a Pharisee named Nicodemus about being born again. Nicodemus could not accept the things of the Spirit of God because he was trying to figure everything out in his head. Thinking in the natural realm, he asked, "Can a man enter his mother's womb again?" The whole idea was foolishness to him. As we read in 1 Corinthians 2:14: "The man without the Spirit does not accept the things that come from the Spirit of God, for they are foolishness to him, and he cannot understand them, because they are spiritually discerned."

In the same way that Jesus was advocating to Nicodemus, I am exhorting us to use our hearts instead of our heads. We can enter the invisible presence of almighty God and a Kingdom that is here only partly, but will come fully in the future. Yet somehow, even while traveling in unfamiliar territory, many in our day are finding the tangible presence of the Kingdom of God.

What can we do to increase the chances of getting a new and fresh breakthrough into this Kingdom?

Don't Protect Yourself!

First is something we need *not* do. In Job 1 we are told that God put a hedge of protection around His servant Job. I would like to believe that the same hedge is available to us today. If we do live with a hedge of protection given to us by God, then we do not need a hedge of self-protection.

I say this because, looking back, I see that in the past I put up my own hedge of protection. I did so to guard myself against being tricked or taken advantage of. What I did not realize was that by hedging myself in, I had hedged God out! In other words I was actually protecting myself against the unseen and sometimes unknown God of the universe. I was so concerned that something might be of the devil that God scarcely had a chance. Eventually I found that my hedge was really useless anyway without the power of God, and what I needed to do was really trust my Father in heaven.

Fortunately I became so hungry for God to move in my life, and for my relationship with Him to become vital reality, that I was willing to risk God's coming to me in new ways. To walk in complete trust with no fear of the unknown was, for me, a major step of faith. Maybe I just began to think, *What do I have to lose at this point, anyway?* I became ready for anything that I judged, to the best of my ability, to be the work of God's hand. It felt as if a huge burden had been lifted off my shoulders when I realized I did not have to analyze and calculate everything anymore.

Ask to Know God's Presence

Next I had to begin asking—and I kept on asking over and over again—that I might know the very presence of almighty God.

Now we all know that Jesus teaches us to ask, and that James says we cannot have if we do not ask. So why did I have to ask over and over again?

Asking over and over may not be a model for every kind of prayer, but in my case I had to separate strong desire from passing fancy. My repeated asking was not only to pursue God but also to test my own level of desire. It is no bother to keep on asking for something we really desire.

Most of us are familiar with Psalm 37:4 that tells us God will give us the desires of our heart. What a wonderful promise! The problem is, most of us have many wants but few passionate desires. Not only did I have to trust as I had never trusted before, and let my requests be known to God, but I also had to commit myself above all else to the most important thing in my entire life. Finally I came to the point where I wanted His all-encompassing presence more than life itself.

Focus on God, Not Self

My next lesson came one day as I was listening to a humanistic preacher who was drenching his hearers with self-centered thinking. Point by point he listed all the things we needed to do to build a better self-image. He said everything our selfish, itching ears wanted to hear. His last point came in the form of a promise: "Promise yourself that you will take time for yourself every day."

Suddenly I had trouble believing that Jesus woke up every day making that promise to Himself. Philippians 2:5 tells us that our "attitude should be the same as that of Christ Jesus." Verse 7 tells us He "made himself nothing, taking the very nature of a servant." Jesus got results in His ministry not only because He walked intimately with His Father, but because He was not living according to self-interest. He was obedient to the point of violent death on the cross. Jesus had no "me" life or "me" time.

Much of the time, by contrast, we believers live a life out of focus with God. We try to do things God's way while not really sure that the ways and words of God are always right. We are trying to walk as His creation while being out of agreement with the Creator.

The ways of God are always right.

Walk in Forgiveness

A final area I found I could not neglect if I wanted to enter God's presence was forgiveness. Our human picture of His love and mercy is shattered if we hold unforgiveness toward even one person. We must forgive everybody, just as God is ready to forgive everybody. Forgiveness is readily available to us, but it does not come by asking alone; it comes by forgiving others. Jesus said, "Forgive and you will be forgiven." He also said, "When you stand praying, forgive." You cannot have unforgiveness toward anyone while expecting to walk with the all-forgiving Lord.

If you ask the average Christian to list the greatest sins, unforgiveness would probably not even make the chart. Yet without giving it, we will not receive it! Without extending it to others, we cannot experience revival or the Holy Spirit's power being poured out today.

You Are Guilty but Not Condemned

While we are on the subject of forgiving others, let's recall our own guilt. I may shock you if I do not follow the traditional thinking and tell you that you should not feel guilty. We often hear a person say that something "makes me feel guilty." The problem is, guilt is not a feeling; guilt is a verdict. You either are or you are not. I hope you are forgiven, but you are still guilty. Whether a criminal feels guilty or not makes no difference when he is standing up in court.

Have you committed crimes against the Kingdom of God? Then you are guilty. Have you fallen short of the glory of God? Then you are guilty.

Like you, I have spent a good portion of my Christian walk trying not to feel guilty. Like you, no matter how many times I was told that my guilt was gone, it appeared at just the moment God was calling me to do something for Him! Guilt is a robber of faith; as with Adam, it causes us to look around for a bush to hide behind. If we are ever to have a real move of God, we must deal with guilt.

I have found that trying to tell myself I am not guilty does not work. I finally had to accept God's verdict on my life. Although through the blood of Jesus I was not condemned, I was and will be forever guilty.

The joy of the good news of Jesus Christ is not that it tries to displace my guilt feelings; it is that guilty men and women go free. Guilty people who should be condemned to die are alive and serving the living God. I have come to realize that only guilty people can truly appreciate the mercy and grace being poured out on us.

Everybody is guilty. Guilty people are preaching and teaching. Jesus took guilty men and made them apostles. Guilty followers of Jesus cast out demons. What joy began to flood my soul the first time I stood before the throne of grace guilty! I *am* guilty and Jesus forgives me. I am guilty and Jesus still loves me and talks to me and encourages me to keep on walking with Him. What freedom! Instead of trying to cover my guilt or even get rid of guilty feelings, I stand boldly before the King of kings, a guilty man set free.

You probably already realize that the devil is a liar. Yet there is one time when he tells the truth: He is always ready to confront us with the truth of our sins. How do we handle that? Do we lie and say we didn't do it? No, just agree with the devil's accusations. I admit right up front that I am guilty—and what can he say after that? I say, "I'm guilty but I'm not condemned. You, devil, on the other hand, are also guilty, but you are already condemned to eternal punishment."

You can break the chains of guilt by being guilty and, with thanksgiving, enjoying your freedom to pray and sing and be filled with the same Spirit who raised Christ from the dead. Thus you begin to move with your heart and not just think with your head. You trust and ask and desire and empty yourself and forgive and rejoice that the guilty go free. You want, with all your heart, a clean break from the past. It is time to enter in.

Enter In

What now? You must enter that special place with Him. How? Hebrews 6:19 tells us what it is that "enters the inner sanctuary." What is it? Our hope. This hope must enter behind the curtain, where Jesus has entered. One of the greatest accomplishments of the cross, lost by traditional religion, is the open door to the Holy of Holies. It is not only a real place, but we can actually go there spiritually while still living on this earth. It is an accomplishment that boggles the natural mind, but a very real promise and available not only in heaven but now.

Verse 18 describes which persons may enter this holy place: "we who have fled to take hold of the hope offered to us." This suggests people who have run from the enticements of this world and hurried with hope toward the throne of God. Such an attitude and action produce the kind of hope that enters the inner place where Jesus, who went before, has entered.

For me, reading this passage used to be like reading a dream. It was not a reality or even a possibility. But if we take the Word of God at face value, and seek the Lord with all our hearts, He will be found in us and we will have access to a place that, before Jesus, mere humans could not go.

There is much we need to do to prepare our hearts and minds and souls so we can truly be temples of the living God. His goal is that, after all our prayer and preparation, we will "enter his gates with thanksgiving and his courts with praise" (Psalm 100:4). Jesus is not the faraway Savior; He is the very near Lord. Yet the tiny space that separates us can seem like the Grand Canyon. How can we close the small gap that still exists between us? If we cannot enter the inner sanctuary, Jesus is near and yet so far away!

Training to Hear God

By now Kathy and I and the team of the Smithton Outpouring have prayed for thousands and thousands of people. Experience is a great teacher. Much of the time people are waiting for that one explosive moment when the Holy Spirit comes and overwhelms them. This can be especially true when people hear a story like mine, in which the lightning power of God struck me and all those in the room with a life-changing flame of fire.

To begin at that moment on March 24, 1996, however, is to miss the steps of the journey that brought me there. Yes, it was something I will never forget. It was an event— a moment in time that has changed me forever. Yet many smaller moments led up to that one great second of time in my life.

Jesus often tests the hearts of men and women as their journey toward Him begins and intensifies. We would all like Him to come as a mighty, rushing wind. And sometimes He does. But God's goal is to give us more than a one-time event. He intends that we learn to experience His presence on a continual basis. To do this we must be trained. Although a rushing wind is good, it takes more training, determination and relationship to hear the still, small voice of the Lord. The key is to be so focused that we notice and receive the very breath of God.

Another way to describe the action of God is waves of glory coming one right after the other in various lengths and strengths. As we attempt to stand in the presence of the Lord, we begin to discern even the tiniest wave and do our best to soak it into our hearts. If God finds a receptive vessel, another wave will follow. Again, we allow the smallest movements of God access to our hearts.

A hard heart cannot accept these tiny waves of glory and will not even notice they exist. That is why personal preparation is so important. Leave the cares of the world behind and open your heart completely to Jesus alone. As you show the Lord your ability and availability as a vessel of His presence and power, the waves will increase in strength and number. Our goal must be to become receptive to every movement of God.

Remember, the 120 met in the Upper Room more than once. What were they doing in the days preceding the great Day of Pentecost? I believe they were doing what I have suggested you do: They were praying, repenting and forgiving. In other words, they met in prepared readiness, receiving everything God had to give, until the mighty wind began to blow. They were all ready, and all received the power of God.

Remember, too, the Bible has promised us the inner sanctuary, and it is not our Lord who is holding back from us. My experience has been that it is lack of preparation and lack of experience that hinders our receiving the glory of God in whatever measure. That is probably why many have come from all over the world just to stand in Smithton in His outpouring power. It is not that we are more spiritual; we simply have more experience. Being with those of experience helps hasten everything in the Kingdom of God.

Isn't that why the house of Cornelius sent for Peter? Technically they could receive by themselves without any earthly help. But lack of experience and some wrong ideas slow the process down. The 120 in the Upper Room had been with Jesus. The house of Cornelius had not. So they sent for someone who had been with Jesus and in the

Upper Room. Smart move on their part—one we could learn from!

So the old biblical principle applies in many areas. Those who are faithful in little will be faithful in much. Work on the areas that soften the heart. Although you may notice only a slight breeze at first, do not give up. The wind of God's Spirit will increase in velocity and intensity.

Longing to Enter

The other night in one of our services, I was standing at the front while we all were worshiping. There were many first-timers in attendance from about twelve states and three countries. I began to sense that the Holy Spirit was about to demonstrate His mighty power in our midst. I was facing the platform but could see over my shoulder that people were leaving their seats and filling up the aisles. By the end of the chorus there were probably 150 to 200 people all around me. Suddenly, as I turned to face them, a surge of power was released in the room, and all those standing fell backward as though a blast of air from heaven had blown in. No one had been touched physically, nor had anyone been pushed down. It was as though someone had yelled *Now!* and on cue everyone joined together in falling to the floor.

I must confess, to the untrained it must have looked as though we had stayed up all night and practiced! Many of those who sat in their chairs looked puzzled, while others looked as if they were thinking, *I wish I had stepped out there.* Many of those touched stayed on the floor for a good thirty to forty minutes.

Immediately afterward I looked down the aisle and saw one lone man and his wife, whom I had never seen before, still standing. It is hard for me to describe the look on this man's face. It was the look of hunger and desire and maybe desperation, all at once.

I asked them both down to the front and watched as they climbed nervously over bodies to get there. Kathy and I prayed for them, not knowing what they desired from the Lord. Moments later they, too, were on the floor—but soon they were up again, and now they looked like two different people.

The woman, who said she had been saved only a few weeks before, began to describe how she had been gripped with something all her life, and for the first time in her life felt free. Her husband told how he had come to the services with pain in his back and neck, but the pain he had learned to live with was gone instantly. More than that, the glow on their faces told everyone present that these two had been with Jesus.

Such are common occurrences to those who long with all their hearts for the Lord to show them how to exit this world, with its false gods, that they might enter the glorious Promised Land of God's divine—and sometimes unpredictable!—presence.

16

Thy Kingdom Come

WHEN we repeat that wonderful line from Jesus' prayer, "Thy Kingdom come," we are saying something profound about our priorities. If God's Kingdom comes, our kingdom has to go. If He is the center of our universe and all we believe, then we must stop putting ourselves in His place.

Ultimately this revival is about Jesus, not about us, even though we may have many wonderful, spiritual moments in God and even though our lives are changed dramatically. Often I find myself coming to God with different complaints. "You know, God," I might say, "I'm trying to preach, but there are some people I'm just not reaching. I'm upset about that." He always tells me, *You're starting to write the story about you again. This isn't about you; it's about Me.*

It would surprise some of us to know that our discouragement is not the focus of Jesus' life. To think of Him as existing to care for all our dysfunctions misses the point. Mark 1:1 says, "The beginning of the gospel about Jesus Christ, the Son of God." When John wrote the book of Revelation, he began with the words "The revelation of Jesus Christ."

The Gospel is not about us, but about Him. It is not about how spiritual we are or are not; it is about who Jesus is and what He has done and what He will do. Jesus did not say, "I have come to follow you." He said, "Follow Me. Live as I live and, if necessary, die as I die." When we start following Him instead of asking Him to follow us, miracles happen. When we pray, fire from heaven falls, blind eyes are opened, the whole world is stirred up and lives are changed!

We must never forget the fact that Jesus loves us and that His love will heal our hurts. My life has been improved tremendously just by knowing Him. But the strength of what is happening in me is not that I am somehow getting better. The change is happening because I am becoming less important in my own eyes. Instead of waking up every morning telling myself how special I am, I wake up every morning thinking, *I'm not nearly as important as I once thought I was.* It is wonderfully liberating!

I count it an honor and privilege to serve the living God because I know that, without me, the world will still go on. Ultimately whether I am in heaven or hell at the end of time makes no difference to God's overall plan. The victory will be won with or without me. If I go to hell, heaven will sing just as loudly. If I go to heaven, hell will burn just as hot. Contrary to the popular humanistic gospel, God is not wringing His hands all day long about how I feel.

We *can* be special—by attaching ourselves to the most special Man who ever walked this earth.

John the Baptist was called the greatest prophet who ever lived, although he did not prophesy nearly so much as the Old Testament prophets and although few of his words are recorded. He lived his whole life in order to conduct a six-month ministry as the forerunner to the

Christ, then went to jail and had his head chopped off for doing what was right.

The greatest apostle, Paul, was forgotten in a prison and said, "At my first defense, no one came to my support, but everyone deserted me. May it not be held against them" (2 Timothy 4:16).

A few months ago I went and saw the actual prison Paul occupied, which has just been discovered. I looked down and wondered how special he felt sitting there in the mud.

And John the Baptist was called the greatest, I think, not because of his preaching but because he knew who he was. Out of knowing who he was, he said those profound words about Jesus Christ that we should all endeavor to live up to: "He must become greater; I must become less" (John 3:30). This is what the Kingdom is about: leaving behind our very lives and allowing Christ to live through us.

Right now many churches are fighting a battle they cannot win because they are fighting in the flesh. But God is raising up a chosen Church birthed by the Holy Spirit, and she will win the war. We will go from being victims to victors, from weak to strong, from divided to united, from lazy to loyal. Jesus will remove the fingerprints of the world that cover us and give us the touch of nailprints. God's people will walk in true humility, true repentance, true joy and true commitment to Jesus, leaving behind cheap imitations of revival.

This is the day of the coming Kingdom, and we must listen for the windows of heaven as they open. God is extending the greatest opportunity any of us has ever received, and I trust that as He continues to speak to your heart, you will traverse beyond what you have known in your Christian life and begin to walk in the power and presence of our King.